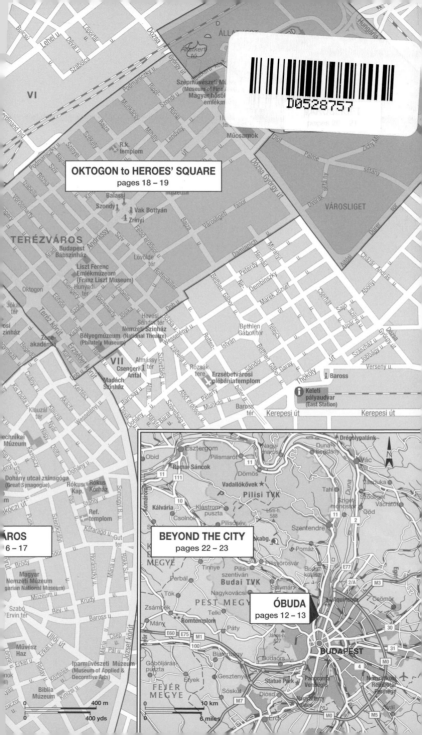

VI

Állatkert
Vidám
tó

Szépművészeti Múzeum
(Museum of Fine Arts)
Magyar hősök
emlékműve

Műcsarnok

R.k.
templom

VÁROSLIGET

OKTOGON to HEROES' SQUARE
pages 18 – 19

Balassi
Szondy
Vak Bottyán
Zrínyi

TERÉZVÁROS

Budapest
Bábszínház

Liszt Ferenc
Emlékmúzeum
(Franz Liszt Museum)
Hunyadi
tér

Oktogon

Hevesi
Sándor tér
Nemzeti Színház

Bélyegmúzeum (National Theatre)
(Philately Museum)

Bethlen
Gáborutca

zinház

Zene-
akadémia

VII

Csengeri
Antal

Almássy
tér

Madách
Színház

Rózsák
tere
Erzsébetvárosi
plébániatemplom

Thököly

Baross

Keleti
pályaudvar
(East Station)

Kerepesi út   Kerepesi út

echnikai
Múzeum

Dohány utcai zsinagóga
(Great Synagogue)

Rókus
Kap.
Rókus
Kórház

m

Ref.
templom

ÁROS
6 – 17

Klauzál
tér

Magyar
Nemzeti Múzeum
garian National Museum)

Szabó
Ervin tér

Múvész
Haz

Iparművészeti Múzeum
(Museum of Applied &
Decorative Arts)

Biblia
Múzeum

0   400 m
0   400 yds

Esztergom
Obid
Pilismarót
Ráchát Sáncok
Dömös
Vadallókövek ★

Nagy-
maros
Duna-
bogdány
Vác
Drégelypalánk

Pilisi TVK

Kálvária
Klastrom-
puszta
Csolnok
Pilisszentiván
Lom-h.
588

Dobogókő
Szentendre

BEYOND THE CITY
pages 22 – 23

MEGYE

Tinnye
Perbál

Pilis-
szentiván
Budai TVK

Nagykovácsi

Tök

Zsámbék
Telki
Mány

Páty

ÓBUDA
pages 12 – 13

PEST MEGYE

Budakalász

Piliscsaba
Pilisvörösvár

Csobánka

Pomáz

Budaörs

BUDAPEST

Romtemplom

PEST MEGYE

Göböljárás-
puszta

Biatorbágy

Etyek

Sóskút

Statue Park

Diósd

FEJÉR
MEGYE

0   10 km
0   6 miles

INSIGHT GUIDES

BUDAPEST
smart guide

APA PUBLICATIONS

Part of the Langenscheidt Publishing Group

Contents

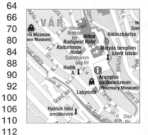

Highlights

▲ When it was built, the **Opera House** was so opulent that the Emperor Franz Joseph was concerned it would outdo Vienna's.

▶ The **National Museum** is Hungary's largest museum and documents the history of the country.

▲ **Hungarian cuisine** has its own unique flavours; visit a grand café and try goulash at one of the city's excellent restaurants.

◀ The outdoor pools of the **Széchenyi Thermal Baths** are hot enough for people to bathe even in midwinter.

▲ Hungary's vast **Parliament** exhibits the crown jewels of St Stephen, the country's founder.

◀ **Buda Royal Palace** now accommodates museums and the Széchenyi National Library.

Budapest

Occupying perhaps the most dramatic setting of any European capital, Budapest combines river, bridges and islands, hills, parks and squares, castles, palaces and churches. And where else could visitors find such an array of museums, feast on goulash, schnitzels and pancakes, and laze the afternoons away in the opulent surroundings of a thermal spa?

Budapest Facts and Figures

City population: **1.7 million**
Population density: **3,261 inhabitants per sq km**
City area: **525 sq km (203 sq miles)**
Number of districts within Budapest: **23**
Life expectancy: **68 years (men), 77 years (women)**
Time zone: **Central European time: GMT + 1 hour, summer time GMT + 2 hours**
Unesco World Heritage Sites: **3**
Number of thermal springs: **80**
Number of thermal baths: **31**
Number of Michelin-starred restaurants: **1**

FORGING BUDAPEST'S IDENTITY

Budapest has gone through many changes of regime over the centuries, with periods of Turkish, Habsburg, Nazi and Communist domination among various others. The look of the city today owes most, however, to the long period when Hungary was part of the Habsburg Empire, and in particular to the later 19th century when prosperity and growing national confidence coincided.

The culmination of this golden age came in 1896 with the celebration of the thousandth anniversary of the founding of the nation. A year of events showcased new building projects such as Heroes' Square and the avenue leading up to it, the dramatically revamped City Park and numerous exhibitions of Hungarian industrial and cultural excellence.

DISASTERS OF THE 20TH CENTURY

Sadly, the party was not to last, and the 20th century brought one upheaval after another. Following World War I and the collapse of the Habsburg Empire, Hungary gained its independence, but at the cost of losing 72 percent of its territory and leaving about a third of ethnic Hungarians outside the borders of the newly diminished state. During World War II, the majority of the country's Jewish population was sent to the gas chambers, and Budapest itself was ravaged by heavy shelling as the Nazis and Soviets fought out the last months of the war. The aftermath brought dreary decades of Soviet domination, repression and decay.

BUDAPEST'S RENEWAL

Fortunately, the last couple of decades, since the collapse of Communism in 1989, have brought renewal and optimism, and the city has re-emerged as one of the most civilised and beautiful in Europe. The grand spa complexes have been restored to their original glory, fashionable hotels have opened once again, the restaurant scene is rediscovering confidence in its national cuisine,

Below: the Castle District's Royal Palace and Funicular lit up at night.

Above: swimmers luxuriate in the stunning neoclassical surrounds of the Gellért thermal baths.

and the city's youth are enjoying the benefits of freedom of expression and emerging prosperity.

THE CITY'S GEOGRAPHY

Originally, the city of Budapest was, in fact, two cities: Buda on the west side of the Danube, and Pest on the east. In 1873, they were united, along with the district of Óbuda, also on the west bank of the Danube. Today, the city is organised into 23 districts, using a system not dissimilar to the *arrondissements* of Paris.

The Buda side of the city is the older settlement, centred around the Castle District. This limestone plateau has been inhabited since Neolithic times, with caves and hot springs among its natural assets. Much later, the Romans built the town of Aquincum to the north, along with a large military camp for its army. You can still see the remains in what is now known as Óbuda. On the other side of the river, Pest is relatively flat, and follows the street plan laid out for it in the early 19th century. It includes the government and main business and shopping districts, along with several large parks, most of the metro network and the main railway stations.

THE CITY'S DEMOGRAPHICS

The city of Budapest has a population of just over 1.7 million, while the greater commuter area includes about 3.3 million people. The population of the country as a whole comprises around 10 million people. The national language is Hungarian, a Finno-Ugric language unrelated to most other European languages (which are part of the Indo-European group) and distantly related to Finnish and Estonian.

The religious make-up of the country is predominantly Christian, with approximately 75 percent of the population still considering themselves members of its faith. Apart from the sizeable minority who class themselves as non-religious, the next largest group is the Jewish community, with about 100,000 people – less than 1 percent of the population. At the start of World War II the city's Jewish population numbered some quarter of a million. Numbers continued to decline even after the Holocaust as the Communist authorities curtailed freedom of religious expression.

Castle District

The Castle District of Buda was established in the late 13th century by King Béla IV after the first Mongol attacks. Since then – despite the defensive strength of this rocky plateau above the Danube – it has been built up and destroyed repeatedly. King Mátyás made it into a fine Renaissance citadel; the conquering Turks let it fall into decline; the Habsburgs devastated it in recapturing it, then oversaw its reconstruction. Finally, in 1945 – in what was Buda's 31st siege – the Germans held out here for three months. Heavy shelling destroyed the palace and a quarter of the old town. Subsequently restored, the district's unique atmosphere has survived against the odds.

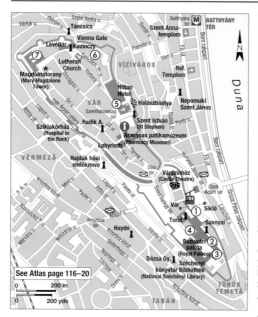

The limestone rock of the Castle District is riddled with caves and tunnels hollowed out by the hot-water springs. For centuries, man has adapted and exploited these for a variety of uses. Today, visitors can enter through a doorway on Úri utca and descend into the **Castle Labyrinth**, a 1,200m (39,300ft) network that has been variously used as storage cellars and bomb shelters. Nearby, on Lovas út, you can also visit the **Hospital in the Rock**, a World-War-II hospital that was later developed into a secret nuclear bunker.

drive into the district unless you are staying at the Hilton Hotel or have a permit.

SEE ALSO HOTELS, P.56; PALACES AND HOUSES P.89

THE APPROACH

Many visitors arrive in the Castle District (or Várhegy) via the **funicular railway** ① *(sikló)*, which runs from Clark Ádám tér below. This old contraption was built in 1870 for clerks travelling daily to the local government offices in the district. As you disembark in Szent György tér, the Royal Palace complex is on the left,

while on the right is **Sándor Palace**, the president's official residence, and, just beyond, the Castle Theatre.

Alternative means of transport to the district include the No. 16 'castle bus' *(varbusz)* that runs between Moszkva tér just to the northwest and Deak tér in the centre of Pest across the river. You are generally not allowed to

ROYAL PALACE COMPLEX

At the southern end of the district is the **Buda Royal Palace**. Not much of it is old: the palace has been destroyed 86 times in its history and what you now see is a post-war reconstruction. While the exterior bears a passable resemblance to its pre war state, the interior is very much 1960s Communist style.

Left: the Castle District battlements offer great views.

On the right-hand side of the square is the **Mátyás Church** ⑤, with its florid tower and roof of brightly coloured tiles. Numerous kings have been crowned here, from King Mátyás in the 15th century to Charles IV, the last king of Hungary, in 1916. In the shadow of the church is a **statue of St Stephen**, who established Christianity in Hungary, and was crowned on Christmas Day 1000. Behind the statue and the church is the **Fishermen's Bastion** (Halászbástya), from which there are spectacular views over the Danube.
SEE ALSO CHURCHES, SYNAGOGUES AND SHRINES, P.36; MONUMENTS, P.66, 68; MUSEUMS AND GALLERIES, P.72

The palace's various wings house the **Hungarian National Gallery** ②, the **Budapest History Museum** ③, and the **National Széchenyi Library**, which contains over 2 million books and several million manuscripts, prints and periodicals.

Access the National Gallery by descending the steps on the Danube side near the sculpture of the mythical **Turul Bird**.

Below: in St Mátyás Church.

For the History Museum and the Széchenyi Library, walk round the back of the palace, past **the Mátyás Fountain** ④ with its assemblage of sculptures, and enter the Lion Courtyard.
SEE ALSO MONUMENTS, P.66; MUSEUMS AND GALLERIES, P.70; PALACES AND HOUSES, P.88

CENTRE OF THE DISTRICT

Walking northwards from the Palace, one of the main thoroughfares of the district is Tárnok utca, lined with historic buildings. On the left is the **Golden Eagle Pharmacy Museum**, and a little beyond that, the Baroque **town hall** (Régi Budai Városháza). At this point, the street opens out into a square, Szentháromság tér, with the **Holy Trinity Column** in the middle, marking those who died in the plagues that struck Buda in 1691 and 1709.

NORTH OF THE DISTRICT

Continuing north on Táncsics Mihály út, the **Museum of Musical History** ⑥ is on your right, housed in the Baroque Erdődy-Hatvany Palace. At the end of the street is a pretty Lutheran church facing on to a small square. On the far side is the old **Vienna Gate**.

Continuing on the road that bears round to the left you see the solitary **Mary Magdalene Tower**. The 13th-century church to which it was adjoined was destroyed in World War II; outlines of its foundations can be seen in the street.

On the other side of Kapisztrán tér is the **Museum of Military History** (Hadtörténeti Múzeum) ⑦, containing relics of Hungary's past upheavals.
SEE ALSO CHURCHES, SYNAGOGUES AND SHRINES, P.36; MUSEUMS AND GALLERIES, P.71; MUSIC, P.81

South of the Castle District: Gellért Hill and Tabán

If you are looking for respite from the crowds of people and the noise of traffic, you don't have to go far in Budapest. The wooded Gellért Hill on the Buda side of the river provides peace, pleasant walks and wonderful views. Just to the north is the sparsely populated Tabán district, with its church, museum, restaurants and parkland, while to the south is one of the grandest thermal bath complexes in the city. Its architecture of beehive domes, lyre balconies and carved geometric patterns is unlike anything else.

GELLÉRT HILL

As well as offering leafy walks with fine views of the city, **Gellért Hill** harbours a number of monuments – ones that pay homage to diverse ideologies. At the very top is the **Liberation Monument** ①, erected in the early years of Soviet domination after World War II. The heroic poses of its idealised proletarians – sculpted in the Socialist-realist style – now seem kitsch rather than inspiring.

Equally unmissable on the hilltop is the **Citadel**, built by the Habsburgs as a fortress and artillery emplacement to intimidate the city-dwellers below after the failed Hungarian War of Independence of 1848–9. This vast hulk of masonry now accommodates an exhibition, a café and a hostel-cum-hotel.

On the side of the hill facing the Danube, there is a **monument to St Gellért** ②. It marks the spot where Gellért was supposed to have been murdered in the 11th century. His efforts to convert the Magyars to Christianity were not always welcome, and a heathen

Above: looking out from the vantage point of Gellért Hill.

mob tied him to a cart and pushed it off the cliff.

The winding paths leading south, down the hill in the other direction, present a pleasant stroll through what is known as **Jubilee Park**, originally laid out to celebrate the 40th anniversary of the October Revolution. As you descend towards the Gellért Hotel at the bottom, a turning off the main path takes you to the **Cave Church** ③ (Szikla-templom). This was once the home of a hermit, but was converted into a church by Pauline monks in the 1920s.

SEE ALSO CHURCHES, SYNAGOGUES AND SHRINES, P.37; HOTELS, P.57; MONUMENTS, P.67; PARKS AND GARDENS, P.90

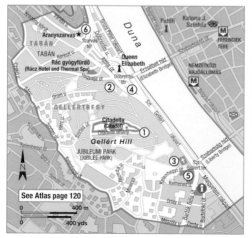

See Atlas page 120

0 ———— 400 m
0 ———— 400 yds

Left: in the atmospheric Cave Church.

The statue of Queen Elizabeth of Hungary in Döbrentei tér pays homage to the Princess Diana of her age. The pro-Hungarian Elizabeth, or 'Sisi', as she was affectionately known, married Emperor Franz Joseph when she was 16, and regretted it for the rest of her life. She was famed for her beauty and fashionable clothes, and went to great efforts to preserve her 50cm (19.5in) waistline (she was near-anorexic). She also had many lovers. In spite of her popularity in Hungary, she was stabbed by an Italian anarchist while on a visit to Geneva in 1898.

THE TABÁN

Once a district of slums, taverns, gambling dens and brothels, the Tabán – between the Castle District and Gellért Hill – was redeveloped in the 1930s and is today an airy neighbourhood of parks dotted with historic buildings and crisscrossed with paths.

The area's landmarks include, in the north of the district, the **Semmelweis Museum of Medical History** (Semmelweis Orvostörténeti Múzeum) ⑥, the **statue of Queen Elizabeth** (1837–98) near the Elizabeth Bridge, the Baroque **Tabán Parish Church**, and the **Golden Stag House**, a fine old inn housing the **Aranyszarvas** restaurant. Recently opened, the **Rácz Hotel and Thermal Spa** – with beautifully restored Turkish baths – is also a destination in itself.

SEE ALSO CHURCHES, SYNAGOGUES AND SHRINES, P.38; HOTELS, P.57; MUSEUMS AND GALLERIES, P.72; MONUMENTS, P.67; RESTAURANTS, P.93; SPAS, P.106

THE DISTRICT'S SPAS

The hot springs of Gellért Hill have attracted settlers since Neolithic times. The Romans and Magyars certainly enjoyed the therapeutic waters, but it was the Turks of the 16th and 17th centuries who really perfected the art of bathing.

The recently renovated **Rudas Baths** ④ at the foot of the hill near the Elizabeth Bridge are perhaps the best of the city's old Turkish baths. Shafts of light filter through the slits in the domed roofs on to the steaming pools underneath. Entrance is open to all members of the public for a modest charge.

Another establishment nearby is the **Gellért Hotel and Thermal Baths** ⑤ near Liberty Bridge, the next bridge along. The old Turkish buildings were replaced in the early 20th century with an extravagant complex in the Secessionist style. In the 1920s and '30s, the lavish interiors with mosaics and chandeliers played host to European high society. Today, in addition to the thermal pools, swimming pool with wave machine and sunbathing terraces, there is a range of treatments on offer.

SEE ALSO HOTELS, P.57; SPAS, P.106

Below: a statue of the beloved 'Sisi' in Tabán.

North of the Castle District: Víziváros, Rozsadomb and Margaret Island

Baroque architecture in Víziváros, thermal spas in Rozsadomb and the parkland of Margaret Island are among the attractions to the north of the Castle District. There are also many layers of history from medieval monastic ruins to the communist ruling classes' suburban villas. To the west, as the city thins, are the Buda Hills, part of a preservationist national park.

0   200 m
0   200 yds   **See Atlas p116**

THE VÍZIVÁROS DISTRICT: BATTHYÁNY SQUARE

Daily life in Víziváros – or 'Watertown', sandwiched between the Castle District and the Danube – is orientated around **Batthyány Square**. As well as forming a minor hub for metro, tram and bus routes, it is the location of a number of important historic buildings.

Chief among these is **St Anne's Church** ①, a twin-towered Baroque church with a fine interior. The church organ is one of the best in the country, and is regularly used for recitals. On the west side of the square at No. 4 is the former **White Cross Inn** where Casanova is supposed to have stayed while taking the waters nearby, while on the north side, the imposing red building is a former Franciscan monastery, which was later converted into a hospital by the Nuns of St Elizabeth. **St Elizabeth Parish Church** can be accessed round the side on Fő utca.

SEE ALSO CHURCHES, SYNAGOGUES AND SHRINES, P.38

THE VÍZIVÁROS DISTRICT: NORTH

Continuing north up Fő utca you soon come to the

> In a genteel surburb of Rozsadomb is the former home of composer Béla Bartók (1881–1945). Visitors can see his study, his collection of beetles, his pianos and even some of the cigarettes (he was a notorious chain-smoker) found inside them when they were being restored. There are also regular concerts of his music.

Király Baths ② on your left at No. 84. The domed Turkish sections of the complex were completed around 1570, while the neoclassical facade is early 19th century. Inside is a large steamy octagonal pool and a series of smaller pools ranging in temperature from extremely hot to icy cold.

Outside, turn left down Ganz utca (by the Baroque church of St Florian) and at the end of the street you will find the **Foundry Museum** (Öntödei Múzeum), dedicated to a slice of industrial history that enabled the construction of Hungary's remarkable railway network in the latter half of the 19th century.

SEE ALSO MUSEUMS AND GALLERIES, P.72; SPAS, P.107

ROZSADOMB

To the north and west of Víziváros are the leafy climes of Rozsadomb ('Rose Hill'), the favoured residential district of party officials during the Communist era. Its inhabitants supposedly had a life expectancy on a par with Austrians while the rest of the city was on a par with Syria. Much of the area

Left: Margaret Bridge connects the island to the city.

ruins of medieval religious houses, many visitors come here today for the bathing facilities. In the southwest of the island are the **Alfréd Hajós Swimming Baths**, named after the double Olympic gold medallist who was also an architect and designed this building. A little further up, but also on the west side, are the vast open-air **Palatinus Baths**, fed by hot springs.

Right up at the northern end of the island beyond the **Water Tower** ⑤ is the thermal bathing complex of the **Danubius Health Spa Resort and Grand Hotel** ⑥. The same springs that feed the baths also provide the right conditions for the nearby Japanese Gardens. A little further north still is the **Bodor Musical Well**, which plays on the hour.
SEE ALSO HOTELS, P.58; MONU-
MENTS, P.68; PARKS AND GARDENS,
P.91; SPAS, P.106; SPORT, P.111

consists of villas, but there are a few landmarks, particularly in its lower reaches towards the Danube.

Gül Baba's Tomb ③ marks a dervish saint from Turkey who died in 1541, is accommodated within an octagonal mausoleum in a tranquil hillside precinct. At river level, to the north, are the **Lukács Baths** ④, a complex that includes ther-

Below: Margaret Island is a parkland haven in Budapest.

mal baths, swimming pools and a drinking cure hall. Next door are the **Komjádi-Császár baths** and **hotel**, occupying an imposing mid-19th-century convent.
SEE ALSO CHURCHES, SYNAGOGUES
AND SHRINES, P.38; HOTELS, P.58;
SPAS, P.108

MARGARET ISLAND (MARGIT-SZIGET)

This island in the Danube is named after St Margaret, who, in the 13th century, lived in a nunnery here after her father, King Béla IV, had pledged her to holy orders if he achieved success in driving away Mongol invaders. The island assumed its present function as a park in the late 18th century; it opened to the public in 1869. The only access then was by boat, until a connection to the Margaret Bridge was built in 1900.

Apart from the acres of parkland dotted with the

11

Óbuda

The Romans chose Óbuda, to the north of Buda, for their settlement on this stretch of the Danube. Evidence of their stay pokes up in the most unexpected places: a bathing complex in a motorway underpass, an amphitheatre among 1970s concrete residential schemes. Subsequent eras have imposed themselves with aristocratic mansions, some fine Baroque churches, a synagogue and a variety of early industrial buildings. Perhaps, however, it is the Communist era that has made the biggest impression; just visit Flórían tér, with its apartment blocks of epic scale, to appreciate the implacable might of central planning.

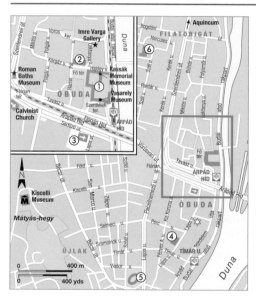

Above: in the Bath Museum.

dedicated to the works of avant-garde artist Lajos Kassák (1887–1967), and the **Museum of Óbuda**, which charts local history. SEE ALSO MUSEUMS AND GALLERIES, P.73, 74

ZÍCHY PALACE

Many visitors will arrive in Óbuda on one of the HÉV surburban trains that start from Batthyány Square in Víziváros and stop off at the Árpád híd station. The exit from the station brings you out on to Szentlélek tér with a statue of the Holy Trinity in the middle and the **Zíchy Palace** ① on your right. The latter, a large, barn-like mansion, was built for an aristocratic family in the

mid-18th century and now houses several museums. The first of these, with its entrance immediately on your right, is the **Vasarely Museum**, devoted to the works of Viktor Vasarely, a leading light in the 1960s Op Art movement.

Around the corner, you will find the main entrance to Zichy Palace, and from inside the courtyard you gain access to the **Kassák Memorial Museum**,

AROUND FŐ TÉR

Continuing past the Zichy Palace, Szentlélek tér opens out into another square, **Fő tér**. On the far side is the **Fő tér Palace** ②, now used as the town hall, while to the left, at No. 1, is the **Zsigmond Kun Folk Art Collection**. Off to the other side of the square, in the middle of Laktanya utca, you are confronted with Imre Varga's group of statues, *People Waiting*. More of the artist's work can be seen in the **Imre Varga Gallery** at No. 7.

the underpass on the eastern side of the square.

Southeast of Flórián tér is a beautifully restored **Calvinist Church**. Otherwise, the area is a particularly brutal example of Communist-era town planning, with vast blocks of flats carved up by busy roads. A few minutes' walk to the north, however, there are more remains, this time of the **Hercules Villa** ⑥, once the home of a high-ranking Roman official, and possessed of some extraordinary mosaics.
SEE ALSO MUSEUMS AND GALLERIES, P.73

AQUINCUM

A few stops to the north on the HÉV train is the **Aquincum Roman Site and Museum**, where the civilian town of Aquincum was founded in 35BC. At its height, 40,000 people lived here, and the ruins of their houses, temples, aqueducts, public baths and amphitheatre can be seen, courtesy of excavations in the 19th century. Inside the museum building are sarcophagi, mosaics, and even a water-powered organ.
SEE ALSO MUSEUMS AND GALLERIES, P.73

On Mátyás Hill, in the east of Óbuda, is the **Kiscelli Museum**, housed in a former monastery built by the Zíchy family in the mid-18th century. The collection comprises Hungarian paintings and sculptures, mostly from the 19th to 20th centuries. There is also a ruined church (bombed in World War II) and fine gardens.

SEE ALSO MUSEUMS AND GALLERIES, P.73, 74

SOUTH OF THE DISTRICT

To the south of Szentlélek tér and the Árpád Bridge runs Lajos utca. Just near the bridge is the large, Baroque **Óbuda Parish Church** ③, while a little further south, the neoclassical **Óbuda Synagogue** can be found on your left. On the other side of the road at Nos 136–8 is the textile factory established by the Goldberger family in 1784. It closed in 1993, only to be

reopened a few years later as the **Textile and Clothing Industry Museum** ④.

Continuing down Lajos utca, at the junction between Nagyszombat utca (off to the right) and Pacsirtamező utca, you come to the Roman **Military Town Amphitheatre** ⑤, which allowed up to 15,000 spectators to watch the gladiatorial contests.
SEE ALSO CHURCHES, SYNAGOGUES AND SHRINES, P.38, 39; MONUMENTS, P.68; MUSEUMS AND GALLERIES, P.74

FLÓRIÁN TÉR

Away to the west of Szentlélek tér, you come to **Flórián tér**. In Roman times, this was the location of a military town where 6,000 soldiers and some of their families lived. The remains of the town's baths can be seen at the Roman **Bath Museum**, located within

Below: ruins at Aquincum.

13

Lipótváros

Lipótváros, or 'Leopold's Town' – named after Habsburg Emperor Leopold II – is the government district of Budapest. Its layout and many of its buildings recall a bygone era, in the late 19th century, when the city was asserting itself beyond its status as a mere satellite state in the Habsburg Empire. The parliament, national bank, stock exchange, post office and ministry buildings all protested the capability for self-government. Moreover, the cathedral, opera house and academy of sciences were of such grandeur and opulence that they threatened to put the imperial capital to shame.

KOSSUTH LAJOS TÉR

Ever since the enormous **Parliament** (Országház) ① building was completed in 1902, Kossuth tér has been the focal point of political activity – both official and popular. Most notoriously, during the 1956 Uprising, thousands assembled here to demonstrate against Soviet domination, only for bullets to rain down on them from the rooftops. Some of the bullet holes can still be seen in the walls of the **Ministry of Agriculture** opposite.

Today, in times of greater political openness, large parts of the parliament building are accessible to visitors – indeed, many of the 691 rooms are surplus to requirement, such as the entire upper house. A highlight of the guided tour is a view of the crown jewels.

Another imposing building on Kossuth tér is the former Supreme Court, which is now the **Ethnographical Museum** (Néprajzi Múzeum), with its exhibition of folk costumes, furniture and ceramics.

SEE ALSO MUSEUMS AND GALLERIES, P.75; PALACES AND HOUSES, P.89

LIBERTY SQUARE

Leaving Kossuth tér by Vécsey utca to the south-east, you soon arrive at the **monument to Imre Nagy** ②, prime minister of Hungary during the failed 1956 Uprising. Tried and executed for treason by the Soviets in 1958, he is shown here looking back towards parliament.

Continuing in the same direction, you next come to **Liberty Square** (Szabadság tér). In the middle is an **obelisk** ③ with a Soviet star perched on top. It is one of the very few Communist-era monuments not to have been removed

Below: the dome at St Stephen's Basilica.

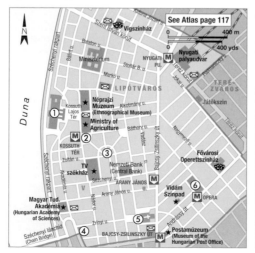

Left: the Hungarian Academy of Sciences.

Seated on some steps, on the south side of the parliament building, is a bronze statue of the poet Attila József (1905–37), probably the most famous Hungarian poet of the 20th century. A quotation from one of his works is set into the stone next to him in raised lettering. It translates as: 'As if my heart had been its very source / troubled, wise was the Danube, mighty force.'

from the city centre. Around the sides are some fine late 19th-century buildings in the Secessionist style, including the former **National Bank** at No. 9 and the old **Stock Exchange** at No. 17. Just off the square at No. 3 Honvéd utca is the **House of Hungarian Art Nouveau**, a beautiful building containing a private museum and pleasant café.
SEE ALSO ARCHITECTURE, P.29; COMMUNIST-ERA HERITAGE, P.43; MONUMENTS, P.68; MUSEUMS AND GALLERIES, P.75

ROOSEVELT SQUARE
Another fine square in Lipótváros, in the south-west corner of the district by the river, is Roosevelt tér. It is dominated on one side by the **Chain Bridge** (Széchenyi lánchíd) and on the other by the **Gresham Palace** ④. The latter is an extravagant Art Nouveau building built in 1907 by

the Gresham Life Assurance Company of London. Today, it is a luxury hotel, though many original features have been retained.

On the north side of the square is the neo-Renaissance home of the **Hungarian Academy of Sciences** (Magyar Tudományos Akadémia). This was established during Hungary's great Reform Period, in the first half of the 19th century, and provided a focus for nation-building endeavours in the arts, science, language and literature.
SEE ALSO ARCHITECTURE, P.26; HOTELS, P.58

ST STEPHEN'S BASILICA
For the city's cathedral, head east from Roosevelt tér along Zrínyi utca. **St Stephen's Basilica** (Szent István Bazilika) ⑤, with its vast dome (which collapsed at one stage during

construction), faces you on its own square. Among the many treasures inside is the right hand of St Stephen, miraculously preserved in a glass reliquary. Each year, on 20 August – the anniversary of St Stephen's canonisation in 1083 – this holy relic is paraded at the head of a procession through the nearby streets.
SEE ALSO CHURCHES, SYNAGOGUES AND SHRINES, P.39

LOWER REACHES OF ANDRÁSSY ÚT
From the back of St Stephen's, it is just a short walk down Bajcsy-Zsilinszky út to the beginning of Andrássy út, Budapest's answer to the Avenue des Champs-Élysées in Paris.

Immediately on your right as you walk up Andrássy út is the **Museum of the Hungarian Post Office**, while a little further up and on your left is the **Hungarian State Opera House** (Magyar Állami Operház) ⑥. This is one of the finest 19th-century opera houses in Europe, with a gilded interior, frescoes and chandeliers.
SEE ALSO MUSEUMS AND GALLERIES, P.75; MUSIC, P.83

15

Belváros

The Belváros, or 'Inner city', is located on the Pest side of the river between the Chain Bridge and the Szabadság Bridge. As well as a wide variety of shops, its streets accommodate numerous historic churches, university buildings and former palaces of the aristocracy. Major sights include the National Museum, the Museum of Applied Arts and the Central Market Hall, with its array of food stalls. To the east of the district is the Jewish Quarter. Apart from the Great Synagogue and the Jewish Museum, its maze of atmospheric streets yields up fashionable cafés, restaurants and shops.

AROUND KÁLVIN TÉR

Kálvin tér was once the site of the old city gates that defined where urban life ended and the great Hungarian prairie began. The square takes its name from the neoclassical **Calvinist Church** (Református templom). It is noteworthy for its stained glass by Miksa Róth and its treasury, containing gold and silver dating back to the 17th century.

Just to the north on Múzeum körút is the **National Museum** (Magyar Nemzeti Múzeum) ①, which charts the history of Hungary. It was on the steps here in 1848 that poet Sándor Petőfi declaimed his *National Song* to the crowds and roused revolt against Habsburg rule.

Another important museum is found on Üllői út. The **Museum of** Applied Arts (Iparmű-vészeti Múzeum) ② is housed in one of the most exuberant buildings by the Secessionist architect Ödön Lechner (1845–1914).

SEE ALSO CHURCHES, SYNAGOGUES AND SHRINES, P.39; MUSEUMS AND GALLERIES, P.77

AROUND FERENCIEK TÉR

North from Kálvin tér is another square that takes its name from its church. Here, it is the **Franciscan Church** (Ferences templom) ③, the venue of many performances by pianist and composer Franz Liszt, who, at times, stayed in the adjacent monastery. On Károlyi Mihály utca, leading south from the square, is the **Károlyi Palace**, which now houses the **Petőfi Literary Museum**. Almost opposite is the looming

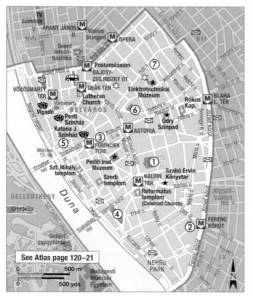

Just a short train ride (on the HÉV line to Lágymányosi híd) to the south of the Belváros is the **Ludwig Museum of Contemporary Art**. Its permanent exhibition charts all the movements of 20th-century Hungarian art, as well as presenting works by the more famous international names.

University Church (Egyetemi Templom), a reminder that this is traditionally a scholarly neighbourhood.

SEE ALSO CHURCHES, SYNAGOGUES AND SHRINES, P.40; MUSEUMS AND GALLERIES, P.76; PALACES AND HOUSES, P.85

VÁCI UTCA

Parallel with Károlyi Mihály utca is one of the city's main shopping thoroughfares. At the southern end of **Váci utca** is the **Central Market Hall** (Nagy Vásárcsarnok) ④, a magnet for those who like their food. Shopping opportunities continue all the way up the street to Vörösmarty Square. There are also many fine buildings along the way, including the little Baroque **St Michael's Church** and the **Serbian Church** on Szerb utca.

SEE ALSO CHURCHES, SYNAGOGUES AND SHRINES, P.39; FOOD AND DRINK, P.52; SHOPPING, P.103

Above: inside the impressive Great Synagogue.

DANUBE PROMENADE

The next parallel street along is the Danube Promenade. The upper reaches are the more interesting, starting from Március 15 tér. Here, you can see Pest's oldest building, the **Inner City Parish Church** (Belvárosi Plébániatemplom) ⑤, founded on the burial site of St Gellért in 1046. The original structure was built with stone quarried from the remains of the adjacent

Left: there are shops and cafés galore on Váci utca.

4th-century Roman fortress of Contra-Aquincum. What is left of this can be seen on the grassy area outside.

Continuing north along the river, you come to the **Vigadó** concert hall. Completed in 1865, it has hosted performances by Liszt, Wagner and Mahler. On the riverfront outside is the embarkation point for **boat trips** up the Danube (see *Beyond the City, p.23*).

SEE ALSO CHURCHES, SYNAGOGUES AND SHRINES, P.40; MUSIC, P.82

THE JEWISH QUARTER

From Vigadó tér, walk back inland along Deák Ferenc utca and you soon come to **Deák tér**. This large square is principally of note as the city's main hub for metro, tram and bus routes. Look out also for the **Underground Railway Museum** (Földalatti Múzeum) in the metro underpass.

On the east side of Károly körút, which leads south from Deák tér, is the Jewish Quarter with its **Great Synagogue** (Nagy Zsinagóga) ⑥. Built in the 1850s, it is the largest synagogue in Europe and can accommodate 3,000 worshippers. To its left is the **Jewish Museum** (Zsidó Múzeum), while behind is the **Holocaust Memorial** in the form of a silver willow tree with the names of victims inscribed on its leaves. Behind this complex, the hinterland of narrow streets, cafés and bars – especially around **Klauzál Square** ⑦ – is well worth exploring.

SEE ALSO CHURCHES, SYNAGOGUES AND SHRINES, P.41; MONUMENTS, P.69; MUSEUMS AND GALLERIES, P.77

Oktogon to Heroes' Square

This stretch of Andrássy út, lined with trees and grand buildings, and culminating in Heroes' Square, was planned to emulate the Champs-Élysées in Paris. As such, its capacity for carrying symbolic meaning has not been lost on the various regimes over the last hundred and fifty years. While the avenue and square were originally built as monuments to Hungarian national pride, Heroes' Square later became the setting for a massive statue of Stalin, and for a time the junctions on Andrássy út were named after Fascist leaders. Today, it is a quarter of smart shops and restaurants, museums and foreign embassies, and has been classed as a World Heritage Site by Unesco.

OKTOGON TO KODÁLY KÖRÖND

The upper half of Andrássy út runs from the crossroads at Oktogon (renamed after Mussolini in 1929) up to Heroes' Square, with Kodály Circus (renamed after Hitler during the war) at the halfway point.

Chief among the places of interest on this section of the avenue is the **House of Terror** ① on your left. This was first the headquarters of the Fascist Arrow Cross Party, and then, after World War II, the Communist regime's secret police. Fascists and Communists alike used the cells beneath the building to imprison, interrogate and torture the ordinary Hungarians they had rounded up. The house is now open to the public as a museum, with exhibitions documenting the atrocities of the recent past.

On the opposite side of the road from the House of Terror are the **Puppet Theatre** for children and the impressive **Academy of Fine Arts** building.
SEE ALSO CHILDREN, P.35; COMMUNIST-ERA HERITAGE, P.42

MUSICAL ATTRACTIONS

Classical music buffs will find this area rich in associations. For performances, in addition to the Opera House *(see Lipótváros, p.15)*, there is the **Franz Lizst Academy of Music** ② on Liszt Ferenc tér, just south of Oktogon. Besides an acoustically-excellent auditorium, the academy boasts extravagant Secessionist decoration.

During the short-lived Hungarian Soviet Republic led by Béla Kun in 1919, the Millennium Monument in Heroes' Square was encased in a red obelisk bearing the image of Karl Marx. After World War II, under another Communist regime, a colossal statue of Stalin was erected on the square's northwestern edge.

On Andrássy út is the Academy of Music's previous premises, with the **Franz Lizst Memorial Museum** ③ on the first floor. The apartment used by the composer himself is preserved, complete with his pianos and personal paraphernalia.

The apartment of another composer forms the **Zoltán Kodály Museum** at Kodály Körönd.

Below: in Heroes Square (left) and the House of Terror (right).

Left: a concert at the Franz Lizst Academy of Music.

1896 to celebrate 1,000 years since the Magyar tribes conquered the Carpathian Basin. At its centre is the **Millennium Monument** ⑥, a tall column with the figure of the Archangel Gabriel at the top. The angel is supposed to have appeared to St Stephen, the founder of Hungary, in a dream and offered him his crown. To the rear of the square are two colonnades containing statues of national heroes.

On either side of the square are large porticoed art museums. To the left is the **Museum of Fine Arts** (Szépművészeti Múzeum) ⑦, housing the national collection of European art. Highlights include masterpieces by Leonardo, Raphael and Velázquez. On the other side of the square, the **Palace of Art** (Műcsarnok) shows exhibitions of contemporary art, many of which are touring.
SEE ALSO MONUMENTS, P.69; MUSEUMS AND GALLERIES, P.78

Unfortunately, at the time of writing, it is closed for renovation until further notice.
SEE ALSO MUSIC, P.80

UPPER REACHES OF ANDRÁSSY ÚT

Before you reach the end of Andrássy út there are two other unusual museums worth stopping off for.

Ferenc Hopp (1833–1919) was a wealthy optician who travelled round the world five times between 1882 and 1914. The **Ferenc Hopp Museum of Far Eastern Art** (Kelet-Ázsiai Művészeti Múzeum) ④ consists of his vast collection of oriental ceramics, sculptures and other *objets* displayed in the setting of his former home. A further array of oriental artworks can be seen at the **György Ráth Museum of Asiatic Art** ⑤, the house of another great collector, nearby at No. 12 Városligeti fasor (on your left as you walk down Bajza utca, off Andrássy út).
SEE ALSO MUSEUMS AND GALLERIES, P.77, 78

HEROES' SQUARE

Andrássy út culminates in **Heroes' Square** (Hősök tere). This was laid out in

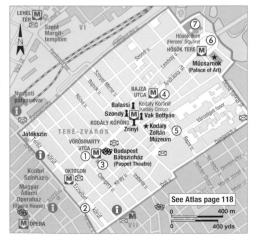

See Atlas page 118

19

Városliget

City Park, or *Városliget*, was originally created in the mid-18th century from an area of marshland known as Ox-Meadow. It was only opened to the public, however, from the early 19th century, attaining its current layout and landscaping as part of the preparations for the Magyar millennium in 1896. City Park was the focus of the celebrations for six months, hosting over 200 pavilions that showcased Hungarian agriculture, industry and culture. A mock-up of a peasant village was built (complete with peasants) and a hot-air balloon offered visitors bird's-eye views of the city.

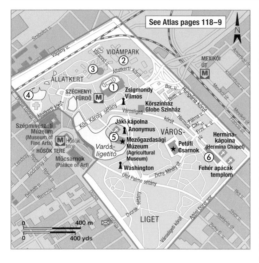

See Atlas pages 118–9

Above: there is plenty to entertain children in City Park.

Just to the east of the baths is a modern glass pavilion, the Szent István Forrás, where you can drink a tankard of mineral water direct from the spring.
SEE ALSO PARKS AND GARDENS, P.90; SPAS, P.109

OVERVIEW OF THE PARK

Visitors enter City Park by Kós Károly Sétány, which leads from Heroes' Square (Hősök tere) and runs through the centre. The first thing you encounter is a bridge (designed by Gustave Eiffel) over an artificial lake. In summer, you can hire boats, while in winter, there is ice-skating. To your right, on an island, you can see the fantasy Vajdahunyad Castle.

Continuing beyond the lake, up the central avenue, you come to the **Széchenyi**

Thermal Baths ① on your

left. If you visit only one bathing establishment during your stay in Budapest, this should be the one. The palatial neo-Baroque complex offers a dozen pools of different sizes and temperatures, as well as a range of treatments, from mud baths to massages. It is, however, the outdoor pools for which the Széchenyi is famous. Even in the middle of winter, the steaming thermal pool is popular with locals, some of whom play chess on floating boards.

ACTIVITIES FOR CHILDREN

On the road that loops round the back of the bathing complex are a number of attractions for children.

First is **Vidám Park** ②, a funfair with over 50 attractions – from an old-fashioned carousel to one of the longest roller-coasters in Europe. Next door is the **Municipal Grand Circus** ③, where you can see clowns, jugglers, acrobats

HERMINA STREET

In the far southeastern corner of City Park is a building with the front of a train emerging from its walls. This is the **Transport Museum** (Közlekedési Múzeum) ⑥, housing a collection of steam trains, trams, vintage cars, motorcycles and bicycles. Nearby, in an annexe known as the Petőfi Csarnok (or 'Hall'), there is also an exhibition on air and space travel. You can find it by retracing your steps just a little way back into the park on Zichy Mihály út. On the west side of the Petőfi Hall is a fenced-off area used for rock concerts – though on Saturday and Sunday mornings it is the venue of a flea market.

Behind the main building of the Transport Museum is Hermina út, lined with grand villas from the city's golden age in the late 19th century. On the far side of the road at No. 23 stands the neo-Gothic **Hermina Chapel**, named after Palatine Joseph's daughter, who died in 1842 aged just 25.
SEE ALSO CHURCHES, SYNAGOGUES AND SHRINES, P.41; MUSEUMS AND GALLERIES, P.79

> City Park is renowned as a rallying point for mass demonstrations. The labour movement has traditionally organised large turnouts on May Day, while during the Communist era crowds were summoned up to engage in dutiful flag-waving for propaganda purposes.

and performing animals, and next door again is the **Municipal Zoo** ④. Entering this last – through a green-domed gateway – you find elephants, giraffes, hippos, lions, crocodiles and monkeys housed in a variety of eccentrically designed enclosures. There is also a beautiful Japanese garden with a Bonsai collection.
SEE ALSO CHILDREN, P.34, 35

VAJDAHUNYAD CASTLE

Another cluster of attractions can be found within **Vajdahunyad Castle** ⑤,

on the island in the park lake. The building itself was deliberately built as a hotchpotch of architectural styles, intended to represent Hungary's architectural variety for the Millennium Exhibition in 1896.

In one wing is the **Agricultural Museum** (Magyar Mezőgazdasági Múzeum), with exhibits on hunting, fishing, horse-rearing and viticulture, while on the other side of the courtyard is the **Ják Chapel**, a pastiche of a 13th-century Benedictine church at Ják in western Hungary. Nearby is the **statue of 'Anonymous'**, the unknown author of a 12th-century chronicle. This monument is famous in Hungary, and many visitors believe that touching his pen will bring good luck.
SEE ALSO CHURCHES, SYNAGOGUES AND SHRINES, P.41; MONUMENTS, P.69; MUSEUMS AND GALLERIES, P.79

Below: the Ják Chapel.

Beyond the City

While there is more than enough to keep visitors occupied within the city of Budapest, those with restless spirits may wish to venture further afield. They are assisted in this by the variety and frequency of public transport services – including trains, the suburban railway (HÉV), trams, buses and boats. And the rewards for the adventurous are many. There are the ancient oak forests and grasslands of the Buda Hills, the relics of the Communist era at Statue Park and the historic towns of Esztergom, Szentendre and Visegrád set amidst the sweeping scenery of the Danube Bend.

STATUE PARK (SZOBORPARK) ①

After the collapse of Communism in 1989, Budapest had a clear-out of its many Soviet monuments and removed them to this park in the southwest of the city.

Here you can find the figure of the Soviet soldier that used to stand beneath the Liberation Monument on Gellért Hill but had long symbolised the opposite of liberty. Here too is the statue of Lenin that factory workers used to mock by placing a slice of bread in the outstretched right hand. Stalin's statue fared even worse. His colossal likeness, which used to stand in Heroes' Square, was toppled during the 1956 Uprising, leaving only the boots behind. A reproduction of these boots is his only remaining memorial.

Other Communist bric-a-brac here includes dozens more statues, numerous plaques and smaller monuments, and what is perhaps the epitome of Communist dysfunctionality – a Trabant

Above: Esztergom sits on the Danube Bend.

car from East Germany.
SEE ALSO COMMUNIST-ERA HERITAGE, P.43

NAGYTÉTÉNY PALACE ②

A succession of castles – stretching right back to Roman times – has been built on this site in the southwest suburbs of Budapest. The palace you see today is a mid-18th-century construction and one of the finest Baroque country houses in Hungary. Following major renovations in recent years, the Nagytétény now functions as a branch of the Museum of Applied Arts, and houses an exhibition of fine furniture from the mid-15th to the 19th centuries.
SEE ALSO PALACES AND HOUSES, P.88

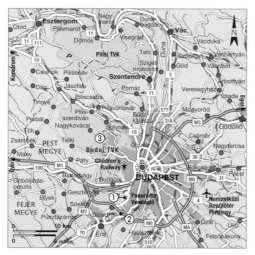

Left: looming Communist monuments at Statue Park.

PassNave (tel: 484-4013; www.mahartpassnave.hu) and **Legenda** (tel: 317-2203; www. legenda.hu) are perhaps the most established operators.

The shortest of the cruises are hour-long city sightseeing tours. Commentary in various languages is available via the headphones provided. In the evenings, dinner-dance cruises are also on offer. These generally leave around 7.30pm and return two hours later. Guests can feast on the buffet-dinner and then waltz to the strains of *The Blue Danube*.

In the summer, day trips are available, taking pas-sengers up the Danube Bend to the historic towns of **Esztergom**, **Szentendre** and **Visegrád**. The trip to Szentendre is only a little more than an hour away, while Esztergom is the fur-thest afield; journeys take four to five hours by boat or around two by hydrofoil.

Further afield still are Bratislava and Vienna. Mahart PassNave operate a hydrofoil service that entails at least one overnight stay.

BUDA HILLS (BUDAI HEGYSÉG) ③

To the west of the city, the Buda Hills – conserved as part of the 10,000-hectare (24,700-acre) Buda Land-scape Protection Area (Budai Tájvédelmi Körzet) – present opportunities for hiking, cycling, observ-ing wildlife and, in winter, sledging and even skiing.

To get there, take tram Nos 18 or 56 from Moskva

tér to Városmajor station. Trains then depart every 20 minutes or so to Széchenyi hegy. From here, you can walk up to the TV tower at the top of the hill or else continue further into the hills via the **Children's Railway**. This narrow-gauge line is staffed by local children, who collect tickets, change signals and make announcements.

Once you are at your destination, there is an abundance of wildlife to spot, with over 100 species of breeding birds and wild boar, fallow and red deer, and several types of snake. If you know what you are looking for, you can also collect wild mushrooms.

DANUBE BOAT TRIPS

Several boat companies operate cruises along the Danube from the waterfront at Vigadó tér just south of the Chain Bridge. **Mahart**

Below: all aboard the Children's Railway!

About 40km (25 miles) north of Budapest, the Danube Bend is one of the most picturesque stretches of the river. The most important of its riverside towns is Esztergom, renowned as the birthplace of St Stephen; it was also here that in 1000 he was crowned as the first Christian king of Hungary. Today, the town is dominated by its cathedral and ruined castle. Of the other towns, Visegrád also has impressive castle ruins, while Szentendre is famous for its many Orthodox churches.

A–Z

In the following section Budapest's
attractions and services are organised
by theme, under alphabetical
headings. Items that link to another
theme are cross-referenced. All sights
that are plotted on the atlas section at
the end of the book are given a page
number and grid reference.

Architecture

A chequered political history has resulted in a heady mix of architectural styles in Budapest. There are the Baroque churches of the Habsburgs, the domed thermal baths left behind by the Turks, and the concrete apartment blocks of the Communist era. Perhaps more than any other, though, it is the exuberance of the Secessionist style that is most associated with the city. In addition to those listed below, see also *Churches, p.36, Communist-era Heritage, p.42, Hotels, p.56, Museums and Galleries, p.70, Music, p.80, Palaces and Houses, p.88,* and *Spas, p.106,* for other important buildings.

Corvinus University of Economics and Management

Fővám tér 8; no admission; tram: 47, 49; map p.121 C2

Built as Budapest's main customs office between 1871 and 1874, this beautifully proportioned neo-Renaissance building was designed with a connection to the railway network, and four tunnels beneath that connected it to the banks of the Danube. In 1951, however, these became redundant, as the building was turned over to a university of economic sciences – at first named after Karl Marx, whose seated statue can still be seen in the impressive atrium. Outside, on the main facade facing the river, are more sculptures: 10 allegorical figures by Austrian artist August Sommer.

Dreschler Palace

Andrássy út 25; no admission; M1: Opera, bus: 105; map p.117 E1

Located opposite the State Opera on Andrássy út, this imposing block

Above: the grand facade of the Dreschler Palace.

was built as apartments for wealthy citizens in 1883. It was designed in the neo-Renaissance style by Gyula Pártos and Ödön Lechner in a departure from their usual Secessionist flamboyance. The building is now home to the Hungarian Ballet Institute.

Hungarian Academy of Sciences (Magyar Tudományos Akadémia)

Roosevelt tér 9; tel: 411-6100; www.mta.hu; no admission; M1: Vörösmarty tér, tram: 2; map p.117 D1

The Academy of Sci-

ences was founded on money pledged by Count István Széchenyi (who also founded the national library and various other institutions in the city). In 1825, he announced that he would forego a year's income from his estates in favour of a learned society for the promotion of Hungarian arts, science, language and literature. On being questioned as to how he would live without money for a year, Széchenyi replied, 'My friends will help me.' This scene is pictured in the bronze relief by

Left: the stately Corvinus University of Economics.

Alpár, after a competition that pitted Austrian and Hungarian architects against each other. The selection of a Hungarian as the winner was treated by the press as a great national victory.

Klotild Palaces and Párisi Udvar
Szabadsajtó utca; no admission; M3: Ferenciek tere; map p.122 B2

At the west end of Ferenciek tere, flanking the road that leads to the Elizabeth Bridge, is a pair of elaborate apartment blocks with floridly sculpted towers. The Klotild Palaces were built in 1902 to designs by Flóris

Barnabás Holló on the side of the building facing Akadémia utca.

During the early years, the Academy had no permanent home, and it was not until 1859 that arrangements were finally made to build one. A committee failed to find a suitable Hungarian architect, so in the end they selected Friedrich August Stüler, the Prussian king's architect, who came up with an extravagant neo-Renaissance design. The completed building

Below: the Klotild Palaces use many architectural styles.

was finally opened in December 1865.

The main facade features statues representing the original six departments of the Academy: law, science, mathematics, philosophy, linguistics and history. At the corners, going from left to right, are scientists Newton, Lomonosov and Galilei, Révai (a Hungarian linguist), and the philosophers Descartes and Leibnitz.

Unfortunately, members of the public are not allowed inside, and the debating hall, picture gallery and magnificent library are the exclusive preserve of the boffins for whom they were built.

Hungarian National Bank (Magyar Nemzeti Bank)
Szabadság tér 9; no admission; M2: Kossuth Lajos tér, tram: 2; map p.117 D2

The ponderous bulk of Hungary's central bank gives a reassuring feeling of permanence if not elegance. It was built in 1905, to designs by Ignác

The Secession style of art and design flourished in the late 19th and early 20th centuries and its products remain a distinctive presence in central Budapest. Characterised by a 'secession' from official and conventional art practices and styles, the movement embraced organic forms, exhibited a taste for the fantastic and emphasised decorative elements. In painting, the major exponents were József Rippl-Rónai, János Vaszary and Lajos Gulácsy, many of whose works can be seen in the National Gallery in the Castle District. In architecture, the style was taken up by Ödön Lechner, Aladár Árky and Károly Kós among others. Mosaic, stained glass, ceramic tiles and wrought iron were all employed in elaborate buildings that could only have been commissioned in a time of prosperity and confidence.

The distinctive style of Ödön Lechner (1845–1914), nicknamed the 'Hungarian Gaudí', is a conspicuous feature of central Budapest. While he owed much to the use of organic forms and iron-framed construction techniques of Art Nouveau architects elsewhere, he also had his own esoteric influences. Fusing Hindu, Turkish and Hungarian folk motifs with European ones, he aimed to establish a Hungarian national style. He is also noted for his liberal use of coloured Zsolnay ceramic tiles. Among his most famous buildings are the Post Office Savings Bank, the Museum of Applied Arts and the Geology Institute *(see Museums and Galleries, p.77).*

Korb and Kálmán Giergl and were named after the Archduchess Klotild, who commissioned them. Intended for use as apartments, they exhibit a wide variety of architectural influences from Renaissance to Rococo to Secessionist.

Next door to the block on the north side of Szabadsajtó utca, at Ferenciek tere 10–11, is another heavily ornamented

building, the Párisi Udvar. Built in 1909 by Henrik Schmahl, the shopping arcade at ground level was designed to emulate arcades in Paris. It features an elegant glass roof and intricate carving in the Venetian Gothic and Moorish styles.

Law Faculty of Eötvös Loránd University

Egyetem tér 1–3; tel: 411-6500; no admission; M3: Ferenciek tere; map p.122 B1

Hungary's largest university – with over 30,000 students – was founded by Archbishop Péter Pázmány in 1635 in Nagyszombat in modern-day Slovakia. It moved to Buda in 1777 and then to Pest in 1784. It was named after the physicist Loránd Eötvös in 1950.

This neo-Baroque building by Sándor Baumgarten and Fülöp Herzog, completed in 1889, was the university's first purpose-built home. It now serves as the law faculty.

Municipal Council Offices

Városház utca 9–11; tel: 327-1000; no admission; M3: Ferenciek tere; map p.122 B3

This, the largest Baroque building in the city, was completed in 1735 to designs by Italian architect Anton Erhard Martinelli, and was intended to house disabled veterans of the wars against the Turks in the last years of the previous century. You can see images of the pivotal victories of the Habsburgs led by Charles III and Prince Eugene of Savoy in low-relief on the gates opening on to Városház utca. The complex was converted and enlarged for use as council offices by Ármin Hegedűs in 1894.

Pest County Hall

Városház utca 7; tel: 318-0111; M3: Ferenciek tere; map p.122 B3

There is a complicated architectural history to this impressive neoclassical building. The facade that fronts on to the street was built by architect Mátyás Zitterbarth Jr between 1838 and 1842. However, by that stage there was already a complex of buildings behind it, including meeting halls, council offices and a prison. During World War II, it was all but destroyed, and what you see today is a reconstruction and adaptation of what was there before. There are now three courtyards inside, the first of which is usually accessible to the public during office hours. Its acoustics make it a popular venue for concerts in the summer.

Post Office Savings Bank

Hold utca 4; M2: Kossuth Lajos tér, tram: 2; map p.117 D2

Left: the Post Office Savings Bank is in Secessionist style.

Right: neoclassical details on the Pest County Hall.

The former Royal Postal Savings Bank represents the epitome of architect Ödön Lechner's Secessionist style. Completed in 1901, this extravagant building combines colourful tiles from the Zsolnay factory, carved folk motifs and a wealth of imagery from the natural world. Look carefully for the bees climbing up to the hives on the gables; they represent industry and prudent saving. The interior, which is usually accessible during office hours, features a grand staircase with wrought-iron balustrades.

Stock Exchange

Szabadság tér 17; no admission; M2: Kossuth Lajos tér, tram: 2; map p.117 D2

Much of the western side of Szabadság tér is taken up by the former Stock Exchange. Along with the National Bank nearby, it was designed by Ignác Alpár, and also completed in 1905. It fulfilled its original function until 1948, when private share ownership was rendered obsolete by the new Communist regime. It subsequently housed the Lenin Institute, and then the headquarters for Hungarian Television. It is now subject to a renovation programme, which will restore the central rotunda and incorporate shops and cafés at street level.

Turkish Bank (Török Bankház)

Szervita tér 3; no admission; M1, 2, 3: Deák Ferenc tér; map p.122 A3

Built to designs by Henrik Böhm and Ármin Hegedűs

in 1906, this building was innovative at the time for its use of reinforced concrete, providing enough support for a large proportion of the facade to be glazed. The gable above is also remarkable, with its colourful mosaic by Miksa Róth *(see Museums and Galleries, p.78)*.

It depicts the Virgin Mary as *Patrona Hungaricae*, flanked by angels and with an assortment of flag-wavers, sabre-rattlers and Hungarian national heroes in the wings. Identifiable figures include Prince Ferenc Rákóczi, István Széchenyi and Lajos Kossuth.

29

Cafés and Bars

The coffee house, or *kávéház*, has played a long and significant role in the social life of Budapest. Over the centuries, writers, politicians, businessmen, lovers and even secret policemen have conducted their affairs over the marble tabletops of the city's cafés. Many of these historic institutions – including the Centrál Kávéház, Gerbeaud and Café Lukács – are still in business, their chandeliers and wooden panelling intact. There is, however, a new breed of café-bar emerging – Szóda and the Sirály, for example – run by a younger generation and embracing today's ethos. See also *Nightlife, p.84* for late-night bars.

CASTLE DISTRICT
Litea Bookshop and Tea-Saloon
Hess András tér 4; tel: 375-6987; daily 10am–6pm; bus: 16; map p.116 B1
For a good cup of tea and a slice of cake, the glass-roofed Litea bookshop-café inside the Fortuna Passage is just the ticket.

Ruszwurm Cukrászda
Szentháromság utca 7; tel: 375-1824; www.ruszwurm.hu; daily 10am–7pm; bus: 16; map p.116 B1
This café-patisserie first opened in 1827 – though there had been

a gingerbread shop here since the Middle Ages. Miraculously, the 1840s Biedermeier interior has survived several wars as well as nationalisation during the Communist era. It is not difficult to imagine aristocratic customers flocking here in the 1900s to buy Linzer biscuits and potcake from the white-moustachioed Vilmos Ruszwurm.

SOUTH OF THE CASTLE DISTRICT: GELLÉRT HILL AND TABÁN
Gellért Espresso €€
Szent Gellért tér 1; tel: 889-5500; www.danubiusgroup.com.gellert; daily 10am–late; tram: 18, 47, 49, bus: 7, 86; map p.120 C2
The entrance to this smart café is just to the left of the main portal of the Gellért Hotel. As well as coffee and cakes, it serves light meals, tapas, wine and cocktails.
SEE ALSO HOTELS, P.57

Left: cake and books at the bright Litea Tea-Saloon.

NORTH OF THE CASTLE DISTRICT: VÍZIVÁROS, ROZSADOMB AND MARGARET ISLAND
Bambi Eszpresszó
Frankel Leó út 2-4; tel: 212-3171; Mon–Fri 7am–9pm, Sat–Sun 9am–8pm; tram: 17; map p.116 C4
The Bambi has not changed since it first opened in 1961. Red vinyl-covered seats, lace curtains, and coffee served in glasses are enjoyed by regulars who play dominoes or chess, and who sometimes look as if they have been there since the 1960s too.

Lánchíd Söröző
Fő utca 4; tel: 214-3144; http://lanchidsorozo.hu/; daily 10am–midnight; tram: 19, 41, bus: 86, 105; map p.116 C1
Traditional local tavern with bent-wood chairs, checked tablecloths and good beer. The owner's enthusiasm for retro kitsch is expressed in the collection of film posters, photographs and old radios.

Left: enjoy grand café ambience at Centrál Kávéház.

Gresham Bar
Four Seasons Gresham Palace Hotel, Roosevelt tér 5–6; tel: 268-6000; www.fourseasons.com; daily 11am–2am; M1: Vörösmarty tér, tram: 2, bus: 16, 105; map p.117 D1
Although the prices are as high as anywhere, the decor and surroundings make this cocktail bar a fashionable place to lounge and chat.
SEE ALSO HOTELS, P.58

BELVÁROS
Bar Ladino
Dob utca 53; tel: 30-874-3733; www.ladino.hu; daily 10am–late; M2: Astoria, tram: 4, 6, trolleybus: 74; map p.118 A1
Although only a recent addition to the Jewish quarter, the Ladino is already very popular. Its laid-back atmosphere, good music and reasonably priced drinks have ensured its success with a young crowd.

Centrál Kávéház
Károly Mihály utca 9; tel: 235-0599; www.centralkavehaz.hu; daily 7am–midnight; M3: Ferenciek tere, bus: 7; map p.122 B2
For those in search of an old-fashioned café

Ráday utca, which runs south from Kálvin tér to Bakáts tér, is lined with cafés and bars, and, is often referred to as 'Budapest's Soho'. Located close to many of the city's university buildings, it is frequented by a young crowd who flock to establishments such as Paris Texas, IF, Soul Café and Jaffa.

LIPÓTVÁROS
Balettcipő
Hajós ut 14; tel: 269-3114; www.balettcipo.hu; daily 10am–midnight; M1: Opera, bus: 105; map p.117 E2
Balettcipő ('ballet shoe') was established by a former ballerina in 1948, and its location near the Opera long ensured its popularity with an artistic clientele. As well as coffee and alcoholic drinks, the café serves light meals.

Café Dunapark
Pozsonyi út 38; tel: www.dunapark-kavehaz.hu; Mon–Fri

Right: the bar at the long-established Balettcipő.

8am–midnight, Sat–Sun 10am–midnight; bus: 15, 115, trolleybus: 75, 76; map p.117 D4
The Szent István Park, just a little way to the north of Lipótváros on the banks of the Danube, harbours this grand and luxurious café-bar. Its first opening, in 1937, proved untimely, but the recent reopening after extensive renovation has effectively tapped the popular taste for retro chic. Take advantage of the early opening for breakfast and the late closing for the cocktail bar or the poker tables upstairs.

31

experience, the Central – with its grand interior and career waiters – is a good place to come. The set lunches, served from 11am until 5pm, are particularly good value, and the house speciality, café pepperino (espresso with chocolate and pepper), is worth a try.

Gerbeaud Confectionery

Vörösmarty tér 7; tel: 429-9000; www.gerbeaud.hu; daily 9am–9pm; M1: Vörösmarty tér; map p.122 A3

Housed within a grand building occupying one side of Vörösmarty Square, this café-confectionery has been an institution in Budapest since it was established in 1858. The interior has chandeliers, fine plasterwork, wooden panelling and marble tables. Outside is a terrace with seating under an awning. Gerbeaud also runs a fine restaurant just around the corner in the same block.
SEE ALSO RESTAURANTS, P.97

Gerlóczy Kávéház

Gerlóczy utca 1; tel: 235-0953; www.gerloczy.hu; Mon–Fri 7am–11pm, Sat–Sun 8am–

Above: the Sirály is situated in a buzzy cultural centre.

11pm; M2: Astoria, tram: 47, 49; map p.122 B3

Recently restored, the Gerlóczy offers a return to the café culture of pre-war Budapest, with mirrors, bent-wood chairs, white table linen and smartly-dressed waiting staff. In summer you can sit on the cane chairs under the awning outside. Food is served throughout the day at reasonable prices.

Sirály Café

Király utca 50; tel: 30-655-0825; www.siraly.co.hu; Mon–Thur 10–8pm, Fri 10am–9pm, Sat noon–9pm; M1: Opera,

trolleybus: 70, 78; map p.118 A1

The Sirály is an institution for modern times, run on a not-for-profit basis as a social and cultural hub for the young, progressive and culturally aware. Its three floors host a lively programme of music, theatre, readings and talks as well as operating as a café and bar throughout the day.

Spinoza Káféház

Dob utca 15; tel: 413-7488; www.spinozahaz.hu; daily 8am–11pm; M2: Astoria, tram: 4, 6, trolleybus: 74; map p.122 C4

The Spinoza seems to offer just about everything. As well as breakfast, lunch, dinner, and coffee throughout the day, there are theatrical performances (May–September only), live piano music most evenings and klezmer concerts on Friday nights (when the restaurant offers a traditional Hungarian-Jewish dinner). The café also hosts art exhibitions.

Szóda Café

Wesselényi utca 18; tel: 461-0007; www.szoda.com; daily 10am–late; M2: Astoria,

Left: go for cake at Ruszwurm Cukrászda (see p.30).

trolleybus: 74; map p.121 D4
The Jewish quarter does a
good line in bars and cafés
that play the latest music
and have a gritty, urban,
hip aesthetic. The Szóda is
one of the most popular.

**OKTOGON TO
HEROES' SQUARE**
Café Lukács
Andrássy út 70; tel: 302-8747;
Mon–Fri 9am–8pm, Sat–Sun
10am–8pm; M1: Vörösmarty
utca, bus: 105; map p.118 A2
The Lukács has had a
chequered history, having
been confiscated during
the Communist era and
becoming a meeting place
for the secret police. However, its old-world decor
and excellent cakes have
now brought customers
back once again.

**Művész Kávézó és
Bisztró**
Andrássy út 29; tel: 333-2116;
www.muveszkavehaz.hu;
Mon–Sat 9am–midnight, Sun
10am–10pm; M1: Opera, bus:

105; map p.118 A1
Located near the Opera
House on Andrássy út, this
is the perfect venue for a
pre-performance dinner or
post-performance drinks.
The café was founded in
1898 and has benefited
from a stylish makeover in
recent years.

**Native Tea House
(Zöld Teknös Barlangj)**
Jokai utca 14; tel: 302-0024;
www.zoldteknosbarlangja.
hu; Mon–Thur 11am–11pm,
Fri and Sat until midnight,
Sun 1–11pm; tram: 4, 6; map
p.117 E2
The 'natives' referred to by
this establishment's name
are the American Indians,
and the building's exterior is
covered in totem poles and
associated imagery. Inside,
you can sample a wide
range of fine teas or repair
to the smoking room for
a connoisseur's choice of
tobacco. Many of the items
on the menu can also be
purchased from the shop.

For a bar with a difference, try
Hat-három Borozó (Lónyay
utca 62; tel: 217-0748;
Mon–Thur 7am–10pm, Fri–Sat
until midnight, Sun 9am–7pm;
tram: 4, 6). Its name means
'6-3', and refers to the score
against England during the
1953 football World Cup. One of
the members of the victorious
side, striker Nándor Hidegkuti,
used to own the place, and
photographs and other
memorabilia associated with
his glory days adorn the walls.

New York Palace
Erzsébet körút 9–11; tel: 886-
6111; www.newyorkcafe.hu;
M2: Blaha Lujza tér, tram: 4, 6,
bus: 7; map p.121 E4
Even if you are not staying
at what is probably Buda-
pest's most expensive
hotel, it is worthwhile taking the opportunity of visiting the café to admire the
architecture, scoff cakes
and luxuriate in the fantasy
of living the high life.
SEE ALSO HOTELS, P.60

Below: soak up opulence and grandeur at the New York Palace.

Children

There is plenty in Budapest to provide amusement for children. There is a zoo, a circus, a puppet theatre, a funfair, and plenty of parks and playgrounds for them to let off steam. Add in the fact that the pace of life is civilised, the scale of the city reassuringly human and that the Hungarians themselves are traditional in their regard for the importance of childhood, and you have a good recipe for a happy family holiday. In addition to the attractions described below, readers should also refer to *Parks and Gardens, p. 90*, for details of children's playgrounds.

Budakeszi Vadaspark

Szanatórium utca, Buda Hills; www.vadaspark-budakeszi.hu; Apr–Aug Mon–Fri 9am–5pm, Sat–Sun 9am–6pm; free; bus: 22 from Moszkva tér

From central Budapest, a 20-minute bus ride and a short walk brings you to the woodland of Vadaspark. Nature trails guide you to the best places for seeing wild flowers and observing birds, and a toy farm (Tue–Sun 10am–noon and 2–4pm) allows children to see cows, goats, sheep, pigs, a donkey, rabbits, chickens and ducks.

Children's Railway

Buda Hills (Buda Landscape Protection Area – Budai Tájvédelmi Körzet); tel: 397-5394; www.gyermekvasut. com; trains run every 45 minutes daily, 8.45am–5.30pm, but check website for any changes; admission charge; tram: 59, 61 from Moszkva tér to the Cogwheel Railway (Fogaskereku Vasut), then to the Szechenyi-hegy terminus and the Children's Railway Station

Above: the Children's Railway is one of a kind.

Two interesting railway journeys snake through tunnels, along valleys and into the glorious scenery of the Buda Hills (Budai Hegység). First the cogwheel train trundles along to the station of the Children's Railway. Then you continue for a 45-minute ride on a narrow-gauge line, with steam trains at weekends and an old diesel locomotive during the week. The ticket collectors, signal operators and announcers of passenger information are all local children aged between 10 and 14 – all, you will be relieved to know, under adult supervision.

Municipal Grand Circus (Fővárosi Nagycirkusz)

Városliget, Állakerti út; tel: 343-8300; www.maciva.hu; shows Wed–Sun at 3pm, also Sat–Sun 11am and Sat 7pm, closed Sept; admission charge; M1: Hősök tere, bus: 4, 20, 30, trolleybus: 75, 79; map p.118 C4

See the strongman, jugglers, a contortionist, clowns, acrobats and performing animals at the permanent home of the Hungarian State Circus.

Left: classic teddies for sale at Babaház.

For toy shops in Budapest, try **Fakopáncs Fajátékbolt** (Baross utca 46; tel: 20 379-8189; www.fakopancs.hu) for old-fashioned wooden toys and board games, **Játékszerek Anno** (Teréz korút 54; tel: 302-6234) for reproductions of old wind-up tin toys and retro paper amusements, and **Babaház** (Ráday utca 14; tel: 213-8295; www.dollhouse. uw.hu) for porcelain dolls in pretty dresses.

Municipal Zoo (Budapesti Állatkert)
Városliget, Állatkerti út; tel: 273-4900; www.zoobudapest.com; daily: summer 9am–6.30pm, winter 9am–4pm; admission charge; M1: Széchenyi fürdő, bus: 4, 20, 30, trolleybus: 75, 79; map p.118 B4

This extravagantly designed zoo is the second oldest in Europe. The elephants live in a Moorish-style enclosure and the snakes and crocodiles in the Palm House built by the Eiffel Company. The giraffes, hippos, bears, lions, zebras, monkeys, seals, polar bears and other animals are similarly well housed and cared for. There is also an aquarium, a petting zoo, a maze, botanical gardens, picnic areas and a restaurant.

Puppet Theatre (Bábszinház)
Andrássy út 69; tel: 321-5200; www.budapest-babszinhaz.hu; daily, usually 10.30am and 3pm, closed July–Aug; admission charge; M1: Oktogon, bus: 105; map p.118 A2

Fairy tales are brought to life at these imaginative children's shows. Although the performances are in Hungarian, the emphasis is on the visual and little is lost if your children are linguistically challenged.

Vidám Park
Városliget, Állatkerti út 14–16; tel: 363-2660; www.vidampark. hu; Apr–Oct Mon–Fri 11am–7pm, Sat–Sun 10am–8pm; admission charge; M1: Széchenyi fürdő, trolleybus: 72, 74, 75; map p.119 C4

With over 50 different rides and attractions, this funfair should keep the little blighters happy for a few hours. There is a 1km (½ mile) -long roller-coaster, the Super-Boat slide, a Ferris wheel, the retro Dragon Railway and the Jungle Fairy Park with rides for very young children. Look out also for the old merry-go-round, built in 1906 and used in the Rogers and Hammerstein musical *Carousel*.

Below: all the fun of the fair at Vidám Park.

Churches, Synagogues and Shrines

As you might expect from a city with such an eventful history, Budapest has a great variety of places of worship, from the Muslim legacy of Turkish rule to the synagogues of a once-sizeable Jewish community. Even for the Christian faith, every conceivable denomination, holy order and style of observance is catered for, whether Greek Orthodox or Lutheran, Catholic or Calvinist.

CASTLE DISTRICT

Buda Lutheran Church (Budavári evangélikus templom)

Táncsics Mihaly utca 28; tel: 356-9736; http://budavar. lutheran.hu; admission for services only; bus: 16; map p.116 B2

This church – of eclectic neo-Baroque and classical design – was built by architect Mór Kollina in 1895–6. It was badly damaged in 1945, and while the exterior was subsequently restored to its original state, the interior was replaced with one of simpler form. On the side of the church is a plaque commemorating pastor Gábor Sztehlo, who saved 1,600 children and 400 adults (mainly Jewish) from persecution during World War II.

Above: the neo-Baroque Buda Lutheran Church.

The **Mary Magdalene Tower** on Kapisztrán tér in the Castle District is all that remains of a 13th-century church that was destroyed during World War II. The outlines of the original building can still be seen in the pavement outside. Even before its final destruction, the building had a rocky history. During the Turkish occupation of the 16th century, it was, for a time, the only Christian church still functioning in Buda. Catholics used the chancel, and Protestants the nave. In 1605, however, it too was converted into a mosque. When the Turks were finally expelled, the church was given to the Franciscans, but then from 1817, it became the garrison church for the troops barracked nearby in what is now the **Museum of Military History** *(see Museums and Galleries, p.71).*

Mátyás Church (Mátyás-templom)

Szentháromság tér; tel: 488-7716; www.matyas-templom. hu; Mon–Fri 9am–5pm, Sat 9am–1pm, Sun 1–5pm; admission charge; bus: 16; map p.116 B1

Despite its name, little of what you see of this church today relates to Mátyás, the great Renaissance king (reigned 1458–90). The first church on this site had been built by King Béla IV in 1255. King Mátyás built a new tower and a royal oratory, and was crowned and twice married here. However, under Turkish rule, the church was converted into a mosque, and during the siege to liberate Buda in 1686, it was virtually destroyed.

The church was later rebuilt in Baroque style – though at the end of the 19th century, it was remodelled by the Romantic historicist architect Frigyes Schulek. The

Left: the Mátyás Church has been rebuilt many times.

SOUTH OF THE CASTLE DISTRICT: GELLÉRT HILL AND TABÁN

Cave Church (Szikla-templom)

Szent Gellért rakpart 1 (near to the Gellért Hotel); tel: 385-1529; daily 9–10.30am, noon–4.30pm, 6.30–7.30pm; free; tram: 18, 19, 47, 49, bus: 7, 86; map p.120 C2

Having at one time been the home of a hermit who cured pilgrims with the nearby thermal waters, the cave was made into a church in the 1920s by the monks of the Order of St Paul. In 1950, however, the church was closed, as the Communist authorities dissolved all religious orders in the country. The monks were taken away in trucks and many of them later executed or imprisoned. The church itself was blocked off with a massive concrete wall.

Fortunately, the collapse of Communism in 1989 brought the restoration of the church to the Paulines and the removal of the concrete wall. A piece

result is a bizarre fusion of Gothic and Art Nouveau.

Sadly, even this has not survived unadulterated. During World War II, tanks battered down the main gates, the roof was burnt, and the building was then used as a stable for Soviet horses. The first phase of restoration was completed in 1970; another is ongoing.

Among the monuments inside are the sarcophagus of Béla III (1173–96) in the Béla Chapel, a gold bust of László (reigned 1077–95) in the St László Chapel, a fine wrought-iron screen separating off the chancel, and impressive 19th-century stained-glass windows.

On the right of the chancel is the doorway that leads up to the St Stephen Chapel and the Royal Oratory. Here you can see the coronation thrones of Franz Joseph and Charles IV, and a replica of the Hungarian crown jewels.

Medieval Jewish Prayer House (Budai középkori zsinagóga)

Táncsics utca 26; tel: 225-7816; www.btm.hu; May–Oct Tue–Sun 10am–6pm; admission charge; bus: 16; map p.120 A4

The Baroque house at No. 26 Táncsics Street was built on the ruins of a 14th-century Jewish prayer house (excavated in 1964). Inside is an exhibition on the Jewish population of Buda in the Middle Ages.

Right: the Cave Church.

of it has been kept as a memento, to the right of the entrance.

Tabán Parish Church (Tabáni plébánia-templom)

Attila út 11; tel: 375-5491; www.taban.t-online.hu; free; tram: 18, bus: 5; map p.120 A3

The Church of St Catherine of Alexandria was founded on the site of a medieval church. The building you see today was largely constructed between 1728 and 1736, though a fire in 1810 and the War of Independence of 1848–9 wrought significant damage. Major restoration was undertaken in 1880–1, when the facade and steeple were given their current form. The frescoes inside are the work of László Kimnach (1890).

NORTH OF THE CASTLE DISTRICT: VÍZIVÁROS, ROZSADOMB AND MARGARET ISLAND

Gül Baba's Tomb (Gül baba türbéje)

Mecset utca 14; Tue–Sun, May–Sept 10am–6pm, Oct–Jan 10am–4pm; admission charge; tram: 17; map p.116 B4

The tomb of Gül Baba, a dervish saint who died shortly after the fall of Buda to the Turks, is located at the top of a medieval cobbled street. His name means 'father of roses', and he is supposed to have introduced the flower to the area. The district's name, Rozsadomb, means 'Rose Hill'.

The octagonal, domed tomb was built between 1543 and 1548 and remains an important Muslim site of pilgrimage. There are spectacular views of the city from the terrace in front.

St Anne's Church (Szent Anna templom)

Batthyány tér 8; tel: 201-3404; open for services only: Mon–Sat 6.45am–9am and 4–7pm, Sun 7am–1pm; M2: Batthyány tér, tram: 19, 41; map p.116 C2

Building of the twin-towered Baroque church of St Anne began in 1740, though was not completed until the 1800s, following funding crises, an earthquake, the dissolution of the Jesuit order in Hungary (which had commissioned it), and a succession of architects.

Inside, the oval-domed ceiling features frescoes of the life of St Anne, painted only in 1928, by Pál Molnár. The church organ is one of Hungary's finest. It was built by Dresden's Jemlich Company in the 1980s and is contained within a magnificent organ case, purchased in 1785 from the Castle District's Carmelite church (long since converted into a theatre). In the summer months, there are regular organ recitals.

St Elizabeth Parish Church (The Capuchin Church)

Fő utca 32; tel: 201-4725; free; M2: Batthyány-tér; map p.116 C2

A church has stood on this site since the Middle Ages, though during the Turkish occupation it was converted into a mosque. Turkish-style masonry can still be seen in the door and window frames in the south wall of the church. The Capuchin monks rebuilt the church between 1731 and 1757 in the Baroque style. In 1785, however, the church and the adjacent monastery were gifted to a healing order, the Elizabeth Nuns, by Emperor Joseph II. The monastery was later converted into a hospital.

ÓBUDA

Óbuda Parish Church (Obudai plébania-templom)

Lajos utca 168; tel: 368-6424; www.peter-pal.hu; Mon–Fri 5.30–7pm, Sun 7am–noon and 5–7pm; free; HÉV: Árpád-híd

The parish church of SS. Peter and Paul was commissioned by the

Left: the Baroque spires of St Anne's Church.

Right: golden detailing in St Stephen's Basilica.

aristocratic Zichy family and built between 1744 and 1749. Inside, there is a particularly fine Baroque pulpit, carved by Bebó Károlynak.

Óbuda Synagogue (Óbudai zsinagóga)
Lajos utca 163; no admission; HÉV: Árpád-híd
Built in the style of a classical temple in 1821 by architect András Landherr. Óbuda's synagogue has, sadly, outlived its local congregation. The building is now used as a television studio.

LIPÓTVÁROS
St Stephen's Basilica (Szent István Bazilika)
Szent István tér 33; tel: 317-2859; www.basilica. hu; Mon–Fri 9am–5pm, Sat 9am–1pm, Sun 1–5pm; free; M3: Arany János utca, Bajcsy-Zsilinszky út
Begun in 1851, St Stephen's took more than 50 years and three architects – József Hild, Miklós Ybl and József Kauser – before it was completed. At one stage, in 1867, the dome collapsed during a storm and work had to begin afresh. Sadly, even after its consecration in 1905, there appeared no end to the troubles. In 1914, a tornado ripped sections of the roof off again; during World War II, the dome was hit by a bomb, which failed to detonate; and then finally, in 1946, a fire brought down the dome again. Reconstruction only began in the 1980s.
Inside, the main altar has a marble statue of St Stephen by Alajos

Stróbl, while on the walls behind are bronze reliefs of scenes from the king's

The densely built-up Belváros district has more than its fair share of churches. There is the **University Church** (Papnövelde utca 9), which was formerly the church of the Pauline monks, who carved the pews, the confessionals and most of the rest of the interior woodwork. Nearby is the **Serbian Church** (Szerb utca 2-4), which, in accordance with the practice of Greek Catholic churches, separates female and male worshippers with a wooden railing. Around the corner is **St Michael's Church** (Váci utca 47b), formerly known as the 'Church of the English Young Ladies' after the Mary Ward Nuns who settled in the adjacent monastery in the late 18th century.

life. Through the doors to the left of the altar is the Chapel of the Holy Right Hand. The right hand in question is that of St Stephen himself, miraculously preserved in a lead and glass reliquary shaped like the Mátyás Church in Buda.
Visitors with plenty of energy can climb the 364 steps of the north tower (open Apr–Oct) for panoramic views of the city. At the base of the other tower is the entrance to the treasury, where you can see an exhibition of 19th-century ecclesiastical silverware.

BELVÁROS
Calvinist Church (Református templom)
Kálvin tér 7; tel: 217-6769; telephone for opening times; free; M3: Kálvin tér, tram: 47, 49; map p.122 C1

39

Right: the Inner City Parish Church is the oldest in Pest.

The neoclassical Calvinist Church was built to designs by József Hofrichter between 1816 and 1830. Architect József Hild subsequently added the porch and tympanum, the pulpit and choir gallery. The building was finished off with its stumpy spire in 1859.

Inside the church, the Calvin rooms feature stained-glass windows by Miksa Róth, depicting figures in the history of Calvinism. The treasury contains gold and silver liturgical objects dating from the 17th to 19th centuries.

Franciscan Church (Ferences templom)

Ferenciek tere 9; tel: 317-3322; http://pestiferences.ofm.hu; daily 8am–7pm; free; M3: Ferenciek tere, bus: 7, 78; map p.122 B2

The Franciscan Church was built in 1727–43 to replace an earlier church that had been converted into a mosque by the Turks and then badly damaged when the city was taken by the allied Christian armies. The building's interior layout replicates that of Il Gesù, the principal Jesuit church in Rome.

Among items of interest inside are the frescoes, some of which were painted by Károly Lotz in 1894–5, while others were executed by Viktor Tardo Kremer in 1925–6. A plaque on the first pew on the right, near the pulpit, commemorates pianist and composer Franz Liszt, who had several sojourns in the adjacent monastery between 1869 and 1871, during which time he put on his famous 'musical mornings'.

Inner City Parish Church (Belvárosi Plébániatemplom)

Március 15 tér; tel: 318-3108; daily 9am–5pm, Sun Mass at 8.30am, 10am and 6pm; free; M3: Ferenciek tere, tram: 2, bus: 7, 78; map p.122 A2

Pest's oldest building, the Inner City Parish Church was founded in 1046 on the burial site of St Gellért. Stones for the original Romanesque building were quarried from the Roman fort of Contra-Aquincum. This structure was destroyed, however, by Mongol invaders in the 12th century. A Gothic replacement was built in the 14th century, though later converted into a mosque by the Turks in the 16th century. A fire in 1723 then burnt it down completely. The church that stands today was built out of the ruins by György Pauer between 1725 and 1739, though this was, in turn, remodelled in the 19th century by Imre Steindl.

Part of the interest, as you look round the church, is to identify the elements related to the different periods in this eventful history. In the chancel, for example, among a row of sedilia round the wall you can see a *mihrab* (prayer niche) from when the church was used as a mosque, while around the back of

Left: praying at the altar in the Franciscan Church.

Above: the Ják Chapel was inspired by a medieval church in western Hungary.

the church is a relief of St Florian, patron saint of fire-fighters, whose protection it is hoped will prevent the building from ever being burnt down again.

Lutheran Church (Evangélikus templom)
Deák Ferenc tér 4; tel: 483-2150; http://deakter.lutheran.hu; open for services only: Sun 9am, 11am and 6pm; M1, 2, 3: Deák Ferenc tér; map p.122 B4
In the corner of Deák Ferenc tér nearest Sütő utca is the Lutheran Church, built between 1799 and 1808. This neoclassical building is simple and uncluttered, both inside and out, as befits Lutheran practices. Adjoining the church is the **National Lutheran Museum** (tel: 317-4173; www.evange-likusmuzeum.hu; Tue–Fri 10am–5pm; admission charge). Its prize possession is the original will of Martin Luther, dating from 1542.

VÁROSLIGET
Hermina Chapel
Hermina út 23; free; tram: 1, trolleybus: 70, 72, 74; map p.119 D4
Designed by József Hild and completed in 1846, this charming Gothic-revival church was built in memory of Palatine Joseph's daughter Hermina Amália, who died in 1842 aged only 25.

Ják Chapel (Jáki kápolna)
Vajdahunyad Castle (Vajdahunyad Vára), Városliget; tel: 252-1359; www.jakikapolna.hu; admission charge; M1: Széchenyi fürdő, bus: 30, 105, trolleybus: 75, 79; map p.119 C4
In the courtyard of City Park's fantasy castle is the Chapel of Ják, modelled on a 13th-century Benedictine church at Ják in western Hungary. The design of the adjacent cloister is based on a variety of sources from the 11th to 13th centuries.

Chief among the synagogues that can be found in the city's Jewish Quarter is the **Great Synagogue** (Nagy Zsinagóga; Dohány utca 2; tel: 344-5409; Mon–Fri 10am–3pm, Sun 10am–1pm; admission charge). Built in 1854–9 by Viennese architect Ludwig Förster in a Romantic Byzantine-Moorish style, it is the second largest in the world outside Israel, with a seating capacity of 3,000. The synagogue's congregation is of the Neolog denomination, which combines elements of Orthodox worship (men and women seated separately) and Reform (use of the organ). Other important synagogues in the Jewish Quarter include the Art Nouveau **Kazinczy Street Synagogue** (Kazinczy utca 29–31) and the **Rumbach Street Synagogue** (Rumbach Sebestyén utca 11–13), which is currently not in use, and is awaiting restoration.

Communist-era Heritage

As the Soviets drove the Germans out of Hungary at the close of World War II, they occupied the country, tightening their hold on power until the People's Republic of Hungary was formed in 1949. Its early years were characterised by Stalinist purges, show trials and indoctrination. Resentment boiled over in 1956 with an uprising that brought the reformer Imre Nagy to power. However, Soviet tanks reasserted Soviet dominance. János Kádár was then leader until the year before the fall of the iron curtain in 1989.

HOUSE OF TERROR (TERROR HÁZA)

Andrássy út 60; tel: 374-2600; www.terrorhaza.hu; Tue–Fri 10am–6pm, Sat–Sun 10am–7.30pm; M1: Oktogon, tram: 4, 6; map p.118 A2

This museum occupies the very building used first by the Fascist Arrow Cross Party – who imprisoned and tortured people here during World War II – and then by the postwar communist regime's secret police, who likewise interned, interrogated and tortured thousands in the cellars beneath the house.

For the reopening of the building as a museum in 2002, the prison cells were reconstructed, and video interviews of survivors are now shown alongside. On the upper floors, there are reconstructions of offices of Communist officials, an exhibition about the show trial of Imre Nagy (prime minister during the 1956 Uprising) and displays documenting the suppression of religious organisations.

KEREPESI CEMETERY (KEREPESI TEMETŐ)

Fiumei út 14; tel: 323-5100; daily 7am–8pm; M2: Keleti pályaudvar, tram: 23, 24, 28

The Kerepesi Cemetery has been the final resting place of Hungary's most famous citizens ever since it was established in 1847. Here, for example, are Lajos Kossuth and Lajos Batthyány, heroes of the 1848–9 War of Independence, slumbering in grand mausoleums.

During the Communist era, the regime's own heroes were added to the cemetery. Chief among these is the red marble grave of János Kádár, Hungary's premier from 1956 to 1988. He has not found the peace he expected: in 2007 the grave was vandalised and his skull was stolen.

Nearby, and now strewn with weeds, is the stone Pantheon of the Working Class Movement, built in 1958. Those killed in the 1956 Uprising are buried in a plot just behind. The plot

Above: the towering Liberation Monument.

for secret policemen, however, is tactfully located on the other side of the cemetery to avert the possibility of scuffles during memorial services.

LIBERATION MONUMENT (FELSZABADULÁSI EMLÉKMÚ)

Gellért-hegy; bus: 27; map p.120 B2

Holding aloft a palm leaf, the towering female figure on top of Gellért Hill is visible from much of the city. The monument was built to commemorate the 'liberation' of Budapest by the Russian army in 1945.

Left: victims of Hungary's regimes are remembered in the House of Terror.

Enormous bronze Stalins and Lenins once loomed over the streets and squares of central Budapest. But with the collapse of the Communist regime in 1989, they, and several dozen of their comrades, were quietly removed to a park in a sleepy suburb.

Here you can find the Soviet soldier that used to stand beneath the Liberation Monument on Gellért Hill *(see left)* alongside statues of Marx, Engels, Lenin, and Béla Kun, leader of the short-lived Hungarian Soviet Republic of 1919. Stalin, however, is represented only by his boots, as his statue was cut off at the knees during the 1956 Uprising.

Other attractions laid on for visitors include a film screening about the Communist secret police, a Trabant car, and a gift shop selling all kinds of Soviet kitsch, from Lenin candles to Red Army medals.

Hidden in caves beneath the Castle District is the so-called **Hospital In the Rock** (Lovas út 4/c; tel: 70-701-0101; www.sziklakorhaz.hu; Tue–Sun 10am–8pm; admission charge; bus 16). It was originally used as a hospital during World War II, but was later converted by the Communist authorities into a nuclear bunker.

Budapest does, however, have a history of recycling monuments in line with changes of regime, and there is an apocryphal, though persistent, story that this one was created originally as a memorial to the son of Regent Miklós Horthy (the far-right ruler of Hungary from 1920 to 1944), who had died in an aeroplane crash in 1942 on the Eastern Front. After the Soviets took control, so the story goes, the sculpture was assigned to a different purpose. Since the fall of Communism, however, some alterations really have been made to the monument: the figure of a Russian soldier and a plaque listing Soviet war dead have been removed elsewhere.

STATUE PARK (SZOBORPARK)

Corner of Balatoni út and Szabadkai út; tel: 424-7500; www.mementopark.hu; daily 10am–dusk; direct bus daily 11am (and 3pm July–Aug) from Deák tér (bus stop with Statue Park timetable), round trip takes about 2 hours, including a visit of approximately 40 minutes; public bus: 7 or 173 to Etele tér terminus, then the yellow Volán bus from gate Nos 7–8 towards Diósd-Érd

Below: the remains of Stalin's statue in Statue Park.

Approaching Szabadság tér (Liberty Square) from the direction of Parliament via Vértanúk tere, you pass Tamás Varga's monument to Imre Nagy, prime minister during the 1956 Uprising. His acquiescence in the Uprising led to his show-trial and execution by the Soviets. His statue stands on a bridge looking towards Parliament and away from the obelisk in the centre of Szabadság tér. This obelisk is one of the few Soviet monuments not to be removed. It was erected in memory of the Red Army soldiers who died in the 'freeing' of the city from the Nazis at the end of World War II.

Essentials

Visitors to Budapest generally find it to be a civilised and not at all intimidating place. Life is lived at a fairly relaxed pace, the city is of a manageable size, and the traffic is nothing like as heavy as in most European capitals. Moreover, the public transport system is easy to negotiate, with a choice of trams, buses, trolleybuses, the metro, and the suburban rail network. All the same, it is good to be well prepared, and this section aims to provide the practical information that will ensure your stay passes off smoothly. If in doubt, the Hungarian Tourist Office has a couple of well-located branches in the city.

CLIMATE

Winters tend to be very cold and sometimes snowy, with an average maximum temperature of 3°C (37°F) in Dec–Feb. Summers are hot and dry; the average maximum temperature is 28°C (82°F) in July–Aug. Annual rainfall is approximately 620mm (24 ins).

CUSTOMS

For the latest official regulations on bringing goods into Hungary, consult: www.vam.hu/loadBinaryContent.do?binaryId=23884. For details on reclaiming VAT on purchases made in Hungary, see *Shopping, p.104.*

ELECTRICITY

The standard voltage from plug sockets is 230 volts, 50 hertz. Plugs have two round pins. British appliances will require an adaptor; American appliances will need a transformer.

EMBASSIES AND CONSULATES

Australia: Királyhágó tér 8–9, tel: 457-9777

Emergencies

Ambulance tel: 104, or 331-9311 for an English-language speaker. Fire Brigade tel: 105. Police tel: 107. General emergencies tel: 112

Canada: Ganz utca 12–14, tel: 392-3360
Ireland: Bank Center, Szabadság tér 7, tel: 301-4960
New Zealand: Nagymező utca 50, tel: 302-2484
South Africa: Gárdonyi Géza út 17, tel: 392-0999
UK: Harmincad utca 6, tel: 266-2888
US: Szabadság tér 12, tel: 475-4400

GAY AND LESBIAN

Although attitudes in Hungary towards gay and lesbian issues are still not as relaxed as they are in Western Europe, major strides have been made in recent years. Not least is the government's introduction of gay cohabitation legislation. The age of consent for gay men is now the same as for heterosexual men, at 14 years. The main support organisation for the gay and lesbian community in Hungary is called **Háttér**, or 'Background' (helpline 06 80 505-605; www.hatter.hu).

HEALTH

Emergency medical treatment is available free of charge on the Hungarian National Health Service to EU nationals and nationals of some other countries within the European Economic Area. Non-emergency treatment must be paid for. Visitors from other countries (including the US and Canada) are required to pay for all treatment, so it is vital to have health insurance in place before arrival.

Budapest also has an American-run **First Med Center** (Hattyú utca 14; tel: 224-9090; www.firstmedcenters.com), which provides 24-hour emergency cover.

INTERNET

Many hotels and cafés have internet terminals, or at least offer Wi-fi access. Reliable, dedicated internet cafés include **Fougou**

Left: some of the best things to do in Budapest are free.

Opening Hours
Banks: Mon–Thur 8am–3pm, Fri 8am–1pm. **Offices:** Mon–Fri 8am–5pm. **Museums:** Tue–Sun 10am–6pm. **Shops:** Mon–Fri 10am–6pm, Sat 10am–1pm. Shops in malls generally open longer, often 10am–9pm. Shops often stay open late on Thursday evenings.

(Wesselenyi utca 57; tel: 787-4888; www.fougou.uw.hu; daily 7am–2am) and **Café Uránia** (Rákóczi út 21; tel: 486-3410; www.urania-nf.hu; daily 11am–10pm). See also www.hotspot ter.hu for a map of access points in the city centre.

LISTINGS
The free weekly listings publications, *Pesti Est* and *Exit*, are released every Thursday. The local edition of *Time Out* magazine (in English) is also very useful.

MONEY
The unit of currency in Hungary is the forint, which is divided into 100 fillérs. For current exchange rates consult www.xe.com. In the future, Hungary is expected to adopt the euro, though it now seems unlikely to do so until 2015 at the earliest.

Visitors can withdraw money via an ATM. These are available outside most banks and operate 24 hours a day. Cards such as Visa, Cirrus and Plus are widely accepted. Alternatively, shop around for the best rates

at the bureaux de change throughout the city centre.

Most hotels, large shops and restaurants accept credit cards such as American Express, Mastercard, Diners Club and Visa.

POSTAL SERVICE
Branches of the Hungarian post office, **Magyar Posta**, open Monday to Friday 8am–7pm. Some also open Saturday 8am–1pm. Stamps ('bélyeg') can also be bought at tobacconists.

TELEPHONES
To call Hungary from abroad, dial +36, then 1 for Budapest, then the 7-digit local number. To call Buda-

Below: a local postbox.

pest from elsewhere within Hungary, dial 06, wait for the dialling tone, and then add the 7-digit number. It is not necessary to use the 06 code if you are calling from within Budapest itself. However, if calling from a mobile, dial 06 in addition to the 7-digit number.

TOURIST OFFICES
The Hungarian Tourist Office is called **Tourinform** (general enquiries tel: 438-8080; www.tourinform.hu); they have branches at Sütő utca 2 (near Deák Ferenc tér; tel: 438-8080), Liszt Ferenc tér 11 (near Oktogon; tel: 322-4098), and at each of the terminals of Ferihegyi airport (tel: 438-8080). There is also a useful tourism office website specifically for Budapest: www. budapestinfo.hu/en.

VISAS AND PASSPORTS
Citizens of EU and most other European countries, as well as the US, Canada, Australia and New Zealand, can enter with just a valid passport (no visa required). Nationals of other countries generally need visas before travelling. Foreign nationals intending to stay for more than 90 days must apply for a residence visa from the Hungarian consulate in their own country first.

Festivals

Wine, pop music, opera, literature, cinema and many of the other good things in life are celebrated with their own festivals in Budapest. When anniversaries of great days in Hungarian history and religious holidays are added in too, the calendar soon brims with interesting activities spread throughout the year. As well as the festivals and events listed below, be sure to check out those in other sections of the book. In particular, see *Film, p.48*, for festivals specialising in animated, arthouse or documentary cinema, *Music, p.80*, for venues and concerts, and *Sport, p.111*, for details of the Hungarian Grand Prix.

JANUARY

1st: New Year's Day
The day after a night of revels is celebrated with a concert of Hungarian popular classics in the Vigadó concert hall.
SEE ALSO MUSIC, P.82

FEBRUARY

First week: Hungarian Film Week
www.hungarianfilmweek.com
Budapest cinemas showcase new Hungarian features, shorts and documentaries.
SEE ALSO FILM, P.49

MARCH

15th: Revolution Day
Commemorates the day in 1848 when poet Sándor Petőfi roused his supporters to start the rebellion against Habsburg rule by declaiming his 'National Song' from the steps of the National Museum. The anniversary is marked with an official ceremony outside the National Museum, while the rest of the city is decked out in the national colours (red, white and green).

APRIL

End of March/beginning of April: Spring Festival
www.btf.hu
Budapest's cultural festival comprises two weeks of events at many of the city's most prestigious venues. The emphasis is on classical music, though there is also plenty of folk music, dance and theatre.

Easter (variable dates)
On Easter Monday men spray women with perfume, with the objective, traditionally, of keeping them looking young and beautiful over the forthcoming year.

MAY

1st: Labour Day
During the days of Communist rule, this was a day of enforced flag-waving. Today, people visit thermal baths or open-air concerts.

JUNE

First weekend: Book Week
www.mkke.hu
Publishers and booksellers tout their new titles during four days of events (many around Vörösmarty tér). Usually, over 1,000 authors are there, signing their works. There are also open-air theatre performances.

Last weekend: Budapest Fair (Budapesti Búcsú)
The withdrawal of Soviet troops from Hungary in 1991 is commemorated with open-air music, theatre and dance events in the city's parks and squares.

Weekends from end of June to mid-August: Bridge Festival
www.fesztivalvaros.hu
In commemoration of its opening in 1849, the Chain

Left: crowds on Chain Bridge for the Bridge Festival.

descend on the city, organising tastings as well as folk-dancing and other entertainment.

OCTOBER
Mid-October: Budapest Autumn Festival
www.bof.hu
Contemporary music and jazz, theatre, dance and cinema as well as a variety of exhibitions.

23rd: Remembrance Day
Public holiday marking the anniversary of the start of the 1956 Uprising, remembering those killed by Soviet-sponsored forces.

NOVEMBER
1st: All Saints' Day
Hungarians traditionally lay flowers and burn candles in the city's cemeteries in remembrance of the dead.

DECEMBER
6th: St Nicholas Day (Mikulás)
On the evening before, children should leave their shoes on the windowsill so that Santa Claus can fill them with sweets and toys.

24th–26th: Christmas (Karácsony)
The Christmas holiday begins at lunchtime on Christmas Eve. It is then traditional to have a dinner of carp, and then on the following days to visit relatives and exchange presents.

31st: New Year's Eve (Szilveszter)
Partying and fireworks celebrate the passing of another year. Public transport in Budapest runs throughout the night.

Bridge is closed to traffic for several weekends each summer. Crowds enjoy music, theatre, watching boat races and fireworks.

JULY
July–mid-August: Budafest
www.viparts.hu
The centrepiece of this music festival is performances at the State Opera.

AUGUST
Second week: Sziget
www.sziget.hu
One of Europe's largest open-air rock festivals, Sziget attracts the young and hedonistic from all over Europe on Óbuda Island. Most camp for the week, and as well as enjoying the music, seek entertainment, enlightenment or just cheap beer at the host of stalls.

20th: St Stephen's Day
After a Mass in St Stephen's Basilica, the patron saint of Hungary's mummified right hand is taken in holy procession in front of the church. In the

evening, a spectacular fireworks display is launched from the top of Gellért Hill.

Last week: Jewish Summer Festival
www.jewishfestival.hu
A week of Jewish music and theatre – principally at venues in the Jewish Quarter – includes performances of klezmer and jazz.

SEPTEMBER
Mid-September: Budapest International Wine Festival
www.winefestival.hu
For about a week, Hungary's top wine makers

Below: at Sziget rock festival.

47

Film

B udapest has plenty to offer visiting film buffs. Many cinemas show English-language films in the original and some even show films with English subtitles. A number of the city's film theatres are historic buildings with interesting interiors – consider booking one of the themed boxes at the eccentrically designed Urania, for example. Then again, there are several cinema bars and cafés which are fun meeting places. Finally, for hard-core cinephiles, there are several film festivals, showcasing everything from animation to documentaries.

HUNGARIAN FILM

Although cinema achieved a foothold in Hungary from the very beginning of the 20th century, the political and economic traumas of succeeding decades hampered the fledgling industry's development. Indeed, many of the best directors of the pre war period (most notably Michael Curtiz and Alexander Korda) left for more fertile working conditions in Hollywood.

Yet, despite wars, changes of regime and censorship, succeeding generations of talented film-makers did emerge, and a handful of Hungarian films have become internationally recognised classics. During the post-war era these have included **Márton Keleti's** A Tanítónő (1945), **Zoltán Fábri's** Merry-Go-Round (1956) and **István Szabó's** Mephisto (1981), while in recent years, perhaps the most acclaimed films internationally have been Hukkle (2002) and Taxidermia (2006) by **György Pálfi**.

ARTHOUSE AND REPERTORY CINEMAS

Bem

Margit körút 5B; tel: 316-8708; http://bemmozi.blogspot.com; tram: 4, 6; map p.116 C4
The cosy Bem has a programme of recent foreign and Hungarian releases as well as a late bar.

Cirko-gejzir

Balassi Bálint utca 15–17; tel: 269-1915; www.cirkofilm.hu; tram: 2; map p.117 D3
This small picture house is run by by cinephiles as a not-for-profit organisation. Its audience of devotees is attracted by the programme of unusual films – the foreign ones are bought in by the cinema's own distribution company – and no doubt also by the offer of free mineral water in summer and tea in winter.

Művész

Teréz korut 30; tel: 332-6726; www.artmozi.hu; M1: Oktogon; map p.118 A2
With five screens, the Művész (or 'Artist') is the city's largest arthouse

cinema. It offers a varied diet of classic and newly-released international cinema.

Örökmozgó Filmmúzeum

Erzsébet korút 39; tel: 342-2167; www.filmintezet.hu; tram: 4, 6; map p.118 A1
Under the auspices of the Hungarian National Film Archive, this cinema screens forgotten gems, classics, cult, silent cinema and documentaries. Films are shown in the original language with, if necessary, Hungarian translation available via headphones.

Szindbád

Szent István körút 16; tel: 349-

Left and **below:** the neo-Moorish Urania National Cinema is grand enough for Hungary's film premieres.

and features. Look out for the nonstop five-hour 'Animated Night' marathons.

Hungarian Film Week (Magyar Filmszemle)

First week of Feb; venues include: MOM Park, Urania National Cinema *(see above)*; www.hungarianfilmweek.com This festival showcases a large crop of recent Hungarian features, shorts and documentaries.

Titanic International Film Festival

Apr; venues include: Örökmozgó Filmmúzeum, Urania National Cinema; www.titanicfilmfest.hu Two weeks of the latest arthouse films, with a jury awarding a prize for the most outstanding and innovative film of the festival.

Verzio Documentary Film Festival

First week of Nov; venues include: Cirko-gejzir; www.verzio.ceu.hu Festival devoted to documentaries on human rights topics from around the world.

2773; M3: Nyugati pu, tram: 4, 6; map p.117 D3 This two-screen arthouse and repertory cinema is one of the oldest in Budapest still in operation. Its programme of mostly Hungarian films is shown with English subtitles.

Urania National Cinema (Uránia Nemzeti Filmszínház)

Rákóczi út 21; tel: 486-3413; www.urania-nf.hu; M2: Blaha Lujza tér; map p.121 D4 Hungary's national film theatre is housed in a 19th-century neo-Moorish palace, which was originally a cabaret, and then a hall for science lectures. Today, this is where Hungarian films have their premieres. Foreign films are shown in their original language with Hungarian subtitles.

MULTIPLEXES
Corvin Budapest Filmpalota

Corvin köz 1; tel: 459-5059; www.corvin.hu; M3: Ferenc körút, tram: 4, 6; map p.121 E2 Interestingly, this impres-

sive cinema building was commandeered by the resistance fighters during the 1956 Uprising. It now screens the latest Hollywood blockbusters.

MOM Park

Alkotás utca 53; tel: 999-6161; www.palacecinemas.hu; M2: Déli pályaudvar As well as showing the usual Hollywood fare, this multiplex also screens opera performances live from New York and Milan.

Palace Kossuth

Váci út 14; tel: 320-4250; www.palacecinemas.hu; M3: Nyugati pályaudvar; map p.117 E3 Shows the latest English-language films in the original language with Hungarian subtitles.

FILM FESTIVALS
Anilogue Budapest International Animation Festival

End Nov; venues include: Urania National Cinema *(see above)*; www.anilogue.com Four days of screenings of European animation shorts

Some students from the Philosophy Department of the Central European University have organised a film club which is open to the public free of charge, and which aims to screen and then discuss films that raise interesting philosophical issues. Films are generally shown on Tuesdays and Wednesdays in the CEU buildings either at Nádor utca 11 or Zrínyi utca 14; check the website (http://philmclub. wordpress.com) for details.

Food and Drink

Hungarian cuisine remains close to its peasant origins, with hearty soups and stews laced with paprika featuring on many menus. Just over a century ago, however, a number of famous restaurateurs brought French tastes, cooking techniques and standards of presentation to bear on the repertoire of traditional Hungarian dishes. Their influence survives to this day, in spite of the intervening grey-mince-and-potatoes Communist years. Indeed, it is a definite strength of Hungarian cooking that its respect for local produce and distinctive traditions has been retained, while foreign influences are admitted only selectively.

BREAKFAST

Traditionally, the Magyar takes his breakfast seriously. A hearty combination of bread, cheese and cold meats might be joined by eggs and even vegetables (bell peppers, tomatoes, radishes and cucumber). If your hotel offers a buffet breakfast, you might expect to find salami, mortadella, liver pâté (*májkrém*), a type of black pudding (*véres hurka*) and Hungarian sausages (*kolbász*).

On special occasions, a breakfast feast is laid on (*villásreggeli* or 'breakfast with a fork'). This is a glorious extravaganza of cold steak, goose liver pâté, caviar, devilled eggs, omelettes, pancakes, fruit and cakes.

Increasingly, however, Hungarians are lapsing into the West European habit of coffee and pastries, toast with jam, cereals and fruit.

Above: Hungarian sausages may appear at breakfast.

It will not escape your notice for long that paprika is used liberally in Hungarian cooking. Grown locally, it comes in several grades (all of which can be purchased at Central Market Hall – *see p.52*), from *Különleges* (Special Quality), the mildest, with a deep bright red colour, to *Erős* (Strong), the hottest, and light brown colour. Be careful, however.

An old Hungarian saying warns that good paprika burns twice. You may find after overindulging that you have a burning feeling in the mucous membranes of the bowels.

LUNCH

The Magyar is always ravenously hungry by lunchtime. To get you going there are soups such as *Jókai bableves* (a bean soup with smoked gammon) or *halászlé* (carp soup with hot paprika), or else pancakes Hortobágy-style (*Hortobágyi palacsinta* – stuffed with minced veal, with a creamy paprika sauce). Then for the main course there could be chicken paprika (*csirkepaprikás* – a stew liberally doused with sweet paprika and cream), Wiener schnitzel (*bécsi szelet*), or the famous goulash stew (*székelygulyás* – a rustic broth of beef, vegetables and paprika).

Dessert will inevitably follow, and high on the hit list will be *Gundel palacsinta* (flambéed pancakes in dark chocolate sauce filled with ground walnuts), *dobos torta* (layered sponge cake, with chocolate buttercream filling and a thin caramel slice on top) and *túrós csusza* (sweetened galuska dumplings baked with túró cheese – similar to quark – often

Left: fresh organic vegetables at Bio-ABC.

pilsener-style lagers these brewers produce – such as the Dreher Classic, Arany Ászok and Kőbányai Világos – are of perfectly reasonable quality.

Hungary is also noted for its fruit brandy or *pálinka*. It is produced from a variety of fruits, hence the Hungarian saying, 'what can be used to prepare jam can also be used to produce *pálinka*'. The most popular, however, is the plum variety, while apricot and cherry are the runners-up. Other distinctively Hungarian spirits and liquors include Vilmos, a brandy made from Williams pears, and Unicum, a bitter liqueur made from 40 different herbs.

with a light custard on top). In the summer there may also be chilled *hideg meggyleves* (sour cherry soup).

DINNER
By dinnertime, the Magyar is flagging, and simpler sustenance is called for. Open sandwiches, a sausage in a roll (*virsli*), bread, cheese and cold meats, or pancakes (*palacsinta*) are popular options.

DRINKS
For alcoholic drinks, as with food, Hungary has its own distinctive heritage. The Romans brought vines to Hungary – or 'Pannonia' as it was then known – and wine has been produced here ever since. There are now some 22 wine regions in the country. Perhaps the best known is Tokaj, in the northeast, which produces a full-bodied white dessert wine. Another famous wine – though, in actuality, of variable quality – is Bull's Blood or *Egri Bikavér*, a dark, robust red wine made from a blend

of three different grapes. Other wines to look out for are the dry red *Kékfrankos* wines from Sopron, the German-style *Olaszrizling* wines from the Balaton region and the sparkling (or *pezsgő*) wines produced by firms such as Törley and Hungaria. Beer drinkers in Hungary are more likely than not to consume the products of one of four large commercial (and now foreign-owned) brewers in the country: Dreher, Borsod, Hungária and Pécs. All the same, the

Below: Hungarian *pálinka* is produced in multiple flavours.

FOOD SHOPS
Bio-ABC
Múzeum körút 19; tel: 317-3043; Mon–Fri 10am–7pm, Sat 10am–2pm; M2: Astoria, tram: 47, 49; map p.122 C2
As well as the organic fruit and vegetables, the soy milk and the herbal teas you might expect from a health-food store, Bio-ABC also stocks organic cosmetics and essential oils – and runs a fresh juice bar next door.

Cadeau Csokoládé Cukrászda és Édességbolt
Verese Pálné utca 8; tel: 317-7127; www.cukraszok. hu; Mon–Fri 10am–6pm, Sat 10am–2pm; M3: Ferenciek tere; map p.122 B2
Visit this artisanal chocolatier for bonbons, fondue and chocolate-covered fruit products – all sold in smart dark-green-and-gold-edged packaging.

51

Right: Hungarian meals are generally hearty affairs.

Nagy Tamás
Gerlóczy utca 3; tel: 317-4268; Mon–Fri 9am–6pm, Sat 9am–1pm; M1, 2, 3: Deák Ferenc tér; map p.122 B3
This is the best cheese-monger in town, with over 200 varieties of Hungarian and imported cheese.

Rothschild
Teréz körút 19; tel: 312-2877; daily 24 hours; tram: 4, 6; map p.118 A2
You can buy all your usual domestic supplies at this supermarket, as well as a range of kosher products.

Stonewall Gourmet
Sütő utca 2; tel: 368-3523; www.stonewallgourmet. hu; Mon–Fri 8am–10pm, Sat 10am–10pm; M1, 2, 3: Deák Ferenc tér, tram: 47, 49; map p.122 B3
Located right in the heart of town, this smart delicatessen sells fine cheese, cooked meats and wine.

FOOD MARKETS
Biopiac
Csörcz utca 18; tel: 214-7005; www.biokultura.org; Sat 6.30am–noon; tram: 61

This open-air farmers' market ensures quality by vetting all producers, and regulating the way the meat, vegetables and drinks are packaged (absolutely no plastic). Some stalls cook up samples of the produce to allow you to test before you buy.

Central Market Hall (Nagycsarnok)
Vámház Fővám tér; tel: 366-3300; M3: Kálvin tér, tram: 2, 47, 49; map p.121 C2
This is by far the grandest of the city's old market halls. It was built in the late 19th century by Samu Pecz with a scale and style of construction that recalls a

railway terminus. There are around 200 stalls beneath its iron-and-glass roof, with, on the ground floor, fine fruit and vegetables, strings of paprika or garlic, cheeses of all kinds, and plenty of good old-fashioned butchery (from chickens' heads to smoked hams to vast numbers of sausages). In the hall's gallery, there are craft stalls, as well as cafés and restaurants. The basement sells fish (including live carp) and pickled vegetables.

Hold utcai Vásárcsarnok
Hold utca 13; tel: 332-3976; M2: Kossuth tér, M3: Arany János utca; map p.117 D2
Located close to Parliament, this charming old food hall sells a range of fresh produce, including fruit and vegetables, meat and cheese.

WINE AND SPIRITS SHOPS
Bortársaság
Batthyány utca 59; tel: 212-2569; www.bortarsasag. hu; Mon–Fri 10am–7pm, Sat 10am–6pm; M2: Moszkva tér, tram: 4, 6; map p.116 B2

Left: *dobos torta*, a popular Hungarian dessert.

Above: a wonderful selection of produce is on offer at Hold utcai vásárcsarnok.

The Budapest Wine Society, established in 1993, has an excellent shop that is stocked with a representative selection of Hungarian wines and spirits, as well as some imported bottles. The society also organises wine tastings.

House of Hungarian Wines

Szentháromság tér 6; tel: 212-1031; www.magyarborokhaza. hu; Mon–Fri 10am–7pm, Sat 10am–6pm; bus: 16; map p.116 B1

Located in a wine cellar converted from part of an old Dominican monastery, this interesting shop stocks 700 Hungarian wines. For a very reasonable charge, you can spend two hours sampling a selection.

Magyar Pálinka Háza Hungarian Palinka House

Rákóczi út 17; tel: 338-4219; www.magyarpalinkahaza.hu; Mon–Sat 9am–7pm; M2: Blaha Lujza tér, bus: 7; map p.121 D4

The Hungarian Palinka House stocks a wide variety of flavours of this quintessentially Hungarian *digestif*, from rose hip to honey to peach to quince.

The Whisky Shop

Veres Pálné utca 8; tel: 267-1588; www.whiskyshop.

hu; Mon–Fri 11am–6pm, Sat 10am–2pm; M3: Ferenciek tere; map p.122 B2

There are over 500 different types of whisky to choose from here, including several that are only available in Hungary.

Zwack Shop

Dandár utca 1; tel: 456-5247; www.zwackunicum.hu; Mon–Fri 9am–6pm; bus: 23, 54

The Zwack company, founded in 1790, is responsible for the strong, dark brown, gloopy herbal liqueur known as Unicum. It was invented by a member of the Zwack family who held the post of royal physician to the Habsburgs. There is now a museum dedicated to the drink, and a shop where you can buy some to take home as presents for relatives. Do have a taste of the drink before you buy a bottle for yourself.

Vegetarianism is not as widespread in Hungary as in Western Europe, but diners can expect to see a few meat-free dishes on most menus. Look out for *lecsó* (a vegetable stew of peppers, onions, tomatoes and paprika), *főzelék* (another stew, made from cabbage, peppers, potatoes, tomatoes, other vegetables and cream, and often topped with a fried egg) and *túrós csusza*, a pasta dish made with cottage cheese and sour cream.

53

History

AD89
The Romans establish a permanent camp in Óbuda for a legion of some 6,000 soldiers.

AD106
Aquincum becomes the capital of the Roman province of Pannonia Inferior.

409
Attila the Hun conquers Aquincum.

600–896
The Avars rule the Pannonian Plains.

896
Magyar tribes led by Árpád conquer the territory of what is to become Hungary.

1000
Coronation of King Stephen and establishment of Hungary as a Christian state.

1046
Martyrdom of Bishop Gellért by a pagan mob.

1241–2
Mongols invade, leaving a trail of destruction. As much as half the country's population perishes.

1247
King Béla IV builds a castle in Buda and makes it his capital city.

1301
The Árpád dynasty ends with the death of András III.

1458–90
Reign of King Mátyás Corvinus.

1526
The 1st Battle of Mohács heralds Turkish rule over large swathes of Hungary.

1541
The Turks conquer Buda.

1686
The allied Christian armies led by Prince Eugene of Savoy drive the Turks out of Buda. The Habsburgs assume power and begin rebuilding the city.

1703–11
Prince Ferenc Rákóczi of Transylvania leads a Hungarian rebellion against Habsburg rule.

1723
The Great Fire of Buda.

1838
Great Flood destroys half of Pest's buildings.

1848–9
A nationalist uprising turns into the Hungarian War of Independence. The Russian army assists the Austrians in crushing the revolt.

1867
The Compromise is agreed with Austria, under the terms of which a Dual Monarchy is created and Hungary gains control over its internal affairs.

1873
The unification of Buda, Óbuda and Pest creates the city of Budapest.

1896
The Magyar millennium is celebrated with a makeover of Budapest and a vast exhibition in City Park.

1914
World War I: Hungary is allied to Germany.

1916
Charles IV becomes King of Hungary following the death of Franz Joseph.

1918
The Austro-Hungarian Empire collapses and Charles IV abdicates. Following the Aster Revolution, the liberal Count Mihály Károlyi becomes Prime Minister. His order to the Hungarian army to disarm prompts the Serbian, Romanian and Czech armies to seize large portions of Hungarian territory with impunity.

1919
March–August: revolution brings Communists led by Béla Kun to power as the Hungarian Soviet Republic. Admiral Miklós Horthy leads a successful counter-revolution and becomes Regent. He retains his position until 1944.

1940
After trying to keep out of World War II, Hungary joins the Axis.

1944
Hungary attempts to withdraw from the war and German troops invade. The Nazis establish a ghetto in Budapest and begin sending Hungarian Jews to the gas chambers.

1945
The Soviet army takes Budapest after a six-week siege. The Nazis had previously blown up all the city's bridges in order to buy time.

1947
Despite losing elections, the Soviet-sponsored Communists tighten their grip over the country's political institutions.

1956
National Uprising is crushed after the Soviet Union sends in 150,000 troops and 2,500 tanks. János Kádár becomes the new head of state, and remains in power until his forced retirement in 1988.

1958
Imre Nagy, Prime Minister during the 1956 Uprising, is executed.

1960s
Reconstruction of the Royal Palace and Castle District.

1968
Hungary adopts 'goulash Communism', introducing limited market-led economics.

1989
After months of demonstrations, the Communist Party relinquishes power. In October the Third Hungarian Republic is proclaimed.

1990
First free elections bring József Antall to power as prime minister and Árpád Göncz as president.

1991
The Soviet army finally leaves Hungary as the Warsaw Pact is dissolved.

2006
Riots break out after the prime minister, Ferenc Gyurcsány, admits to lying in order to win the election. He also admits to having done nothing of any value during the four years of his previous term of office.

2008
Hungary agrees a €20 billion loan facility with the IMF, EU and World Bank after its currency is badly hit in October during the worldwide financial crisis.

2010
Parliamentary elections oust the Hungarian Socialist Party from power, as the electorate appear to blame them for the country's economic problems.

Hotels

Recent years have seen a renaissance in Budapest's hotel industry. Visitors can now choose from spa hotels, self-catering 'suites', historic hotels in the grand style and designer boutiques. Moreover, the competition keeps prices surprisingly low. This has put right some of the ravages of history. During World War II some of the grandest hotels – many dating back to the *Belle Epoque* of the 1900s – were destroyed or badly damaged. The Communist era then brought neglect and poor service. Fortunately, the city's heritage has now been restored, while newly built hotels have injected a shot of fashionable design.

CASTLE DISTRICT
Hilton Budapest Hotel
Hess András tér 1–3; tel: 889-6600; www.hilton.com; €€€; bus: 16; map p.116 B1

The 1970s made its mark on the Castle District with this 322-room, corporate-style hotel. Remarkably, this kitsch hulk incorporates the ruins of a 13th-century Dominican church as well as an 18th-century Jesuit college. Its commanding position above the Danube and the city beyond ensures good views for hotel guests. Business travellers and families are equally well catered for, with a business centre, a gym, a beauty salon and a babysitting service on site.

Price guide for a standard double room for one night, without breakfast, in peak season:

€€€€	over €200
€€€	€100–200
€€	€50–100
€	up to €50

Above: fabulous views from the top of the Lánchíd 19.

Kulturinnov Hotel
Szentháromság tér 6; tel: 224-8102; www.mka.hu; €–€€; bus: 16; map p.116 B1

The Hungarian Culture Foundation offers accommodation within a neo-Gothic palace (built 1904) opposite the Mátyás Church. It is a good choice for travellers on a budget, especially because the price includes a hearty buffet breakfast. Book early to reserve one of the 16 rooms, especially if you are keen to have one with a street view.

Lánchíd 19
Lánchíd utca 19; tel: 419-1900; www.lanchid19hotel.hu; €€; bus: 16, 86, 105; map p.120 B4

Located just a few steps from its namesake, the Chain Bridge, and close to the funicular up to the Castle District, this four-star boutique hotel nestles in a plum position. The designers clearly had fun with their award-winning efforts. The striking exterior looking on to the Danube has glass panes arranged in waves, which change colour according to the season. The 45 rooms all have different design classics and individual artworks, while the three suites at the top of the building have jacuzzi-baths from which you can admire panoramic views of the city. The public areas are decorated with artworks by Françoise Gilot (one of Picasso's wives). And yet, surprisingly, for all this, the prices are very reasonable indeed.

Left: stained glass details adorn the Gellért Hotel.

also have free use of the adjacent thermal-bath complex.
SEE ALSO SPAS, P.106

Rácz Hotel and Thermal Spa

Hadnagy utca 8–10; tel: 266-0606; www.raczhotel.com; €€€; tram: 18, 19, bus: 7, 86; map p.120 B3

Set in beautiful gardens not far from the Elizabeth Bridge, the Rácz is Budapest's newest five-star hotel, officially opened in 2010. The 67-room boutique hotel adjoins a spa complex, which incorporates beautifully restored 16th-century Turkish baths as well as facilities for a wealth of health and beauty treatments. With a restaurant, bistro, lounge and cocktail bar added to the offering, guests may sometimes find themselves too comfortable here to bother venturing into the city outside.
SEE ALSO SPAS, P.106

NORTH OF THE CASTLE DISTRICT: VÍZIVÁROS, ROZSADOMB AND MARGARET ISLAND

Art'otel

Bem rakpart 16–19; tel: 487-9487; www.artotels.com; €€–€€€; M2: Batthyány tér, bus: 86; map p.116 C1

The Budapest branch of this small German chain offers boutique-hotel styling and a wonderful location. Looking out, you have great views of the Danube, and, just above, the Castle, while inside is smart contemporary design embellished with artworks by American artist Donald Sultan. Facilities include

Hotel rates can, of course, vary during the year. Peak season runs from roughly May to mid-September, though other busy times when prices escalate include New Year, the Spring Festival in late March, and around the time of the Hungarian Grand Prix (usually mid-August).

SOUTH OF THE CASTLE DISTRICT: GELLÉRT HILL AND TABÁN

Citadella Hotel

Citadella sétány; tel: 466-5794; www.citadella.hu; €; tram: 18, bus: 27; map p.120 B2

This is a hotel with a difference, set as it is within the massive citadel fortification built by the Habsburgs on Gellért Hill after the suppression of the 1848–9 War of Independence. It offers 12 simple, clean, low-priced rooms, some with fine views. There is also a 14-bed dormitory.
SEE ALSO MONUMENTS, P.67

Gellért Hotel

Szent Gellért tér 1; tel: 889-5500; www.danubiushotels.

com; €€–€€€; tram: 18, 19, 47, 49, bus: 7, 86; map p.120 C2

Situated at the foot of Gellért Hill near the Liberty Bridge, this exuberantly designed hotel and bathing complex is the epitome of late Secessionist style. At night, its floodlit exterior – with its beehive domes and balconies decorated with lyres – is a city landmark. Facilities include everything you come to expect of large hotels – from wi-fi to babysitting services – though in addition, guests

Below: bold design and decor at the Art'otel.

If camping is more your style, Budapest has several sites to cater for you. The largest – and probably the best equipped and most scenic – is **Római Camping**, a little north of Óbuda (Szentendrei út 189; tel: 388-7167; www.romaicamping.hu). Others include **Haller Camping** (Haller utca 27; tel: 476-3418; www.hallercamping.hu) and the centrally located **Biker Camp** (Benyovszky Móric utca 40; tel: 333-7059; www.bikercamp.hu). Campsites are generally open from May to October.

the Chelsea restaurant, a café-bar and a gym. There are 164 rooms in total.

Danubius Health Spa Resort Margitsziget and Danubius Grand Hotel Margitsziget
Margitsziget; tel: 889-4700; www.danubiusgroup.com; €€–€€€; bus: 26; map p.117 D4
These two hotels (both four-star standard) are neighbours on Margaret Island, and are linked by a heated tunnel, which allows guests access to the

facilities of both. The Health Spa Resort – built in the 1970s as the world's first city-based spa hotel – has 267 rooms and is geared particularly to guests seeking medically orientated therapies, such as rheumatic treatments; it is also well equipped for travellers with disabilities or allergies. What the Health Spa Resort has in facilities, the Grand has in style. This 164-room hotel was built to designs by Miklós Ybl in 1873, and has recently benefited from a thorough refurbishment. SEE ALSO SPAS, P.106

Hotel Császár
Frankel Leó út 35; tel: 336-2640; www.csaszarhotel.hu; €€; tram: 4, 6, bus: 6, 86; map p.116 C4
Located on the Buda side of the river near the Margaret Bridge, the Császár occupies an imposing mid-19th-century convent building. The old monastic precincts also accommodate the Komjádi-Császár baths (indoor and outdoor pools – one 50m in length), to which hotel guests have

free access once per day. The 34 rooms are simply furnished, but comfortable.

Hotel Papillon
Rózsahegy utca 3/B; tel: 212-4750; www.hotelpapillon.hu; €; HÉV: Margit híd, tram: 4, 6; map p.116 B4
For a budget stay and a good night's sleep, this friendly little hotel is worth the walk up a hill in the sedate and leafy Rozsadomb district.

LIPÓTVÁROS
Atrium Fashion Hotel
Csokonai utca 14; tel: 299-0777; www.atriumhotelbudapest.com; €€; M2: Blaha Lujza tér, tram: 4, 6, bus: 7; map p.121 E4
This four-star boutique hotel is a bright and breezy recent addition to the city. Its 57 rooms are designed in up-to-the-minute style to give a cheerful and airy feel. Wi-fi and flat-screen televisions are standard throughout.

Four Seasons Gresham Palace Hotel
Roosevelt tér 5–6; tel: 268-6000; www.fourseasons.com;

Below: fans of Art Nouveau will appreciate the Four Seasons Gresham Palace Hotel.

Right: the Kempinski Hotel Corvinus is smart and modern.

€€€€; M1: Vörösmarty tér, tram: 2, bus: 16; map p.117 D1

This magnificent Art Nouveau palace – with original marble, Zsolnay tiles, stained glass and fabulous Secession-style metalwork – was built in 1907. Although it was badly damaged during World War II, it has since been renovated, and opened in 2004 as a magnificent five-star hotel. The 179 rooms have a restrained elegance about them, and many have wonderful views over the Danube. Facilities include a spa on the top floor, the **Páva** restaurant, and the stylish **Gresham Bar**.
SEE ALSO CAFÉS AND BARS, P.31; RESTAURANTS, P.95

Hotel Pest
Paulau Ede utca 31; tel: 343-1198; www.hotelpest.hu; €€€; M1: Opera; map p.117 E1
This independent hotel occupies a handsome 18th-century building near the opera house. Its 25 spacious rooms are simply but smartly decorated, with traditional furnishings and parquet flooring.

K+K Hotel Opera
Révay utca 24; tel: 269-0222; www.kkhotels.com; €€–€€€; M1: Opera; map p.117 E1
A branch of the reliable Austria chain, this hotel is located conveniently for the opera house and theatre district. The interior is stylishly designed, and facilities include a business centre, a gym and underground parking.

Kempinski Hotel Corvinus
Erzsébet tér 7–8; tel: 429-3777; www.kempinski-budapest.com; €€–€€€; M1, 2, 3: Deák Ferenc tér; map p.122 A4
Located in an impersonal corporate glass building built in the 1990s, the upmarket Corvinus offers 335 executive bedrooms, all furnished in a way that should make any salaryman feel at home. Facilities include a swimming pool, a fitness centre, an Asian-style spa and a business centre.

Marmara Hotel
Nagy Ignác utca 21; tel: 501-9100; www.marmara.hu; €€; M3: Nyugati pu.; map p.117 E3
This 93-room boutique hotel is newly built and has been designed with great attention to detail. It seems every surface has been upholstered or covered in some plush finish, and the warm but restrained colours of the decor enhance the feeling of comfort and calm.

Below: luxurious furnishings at the Marmara Hotel.

Price guide for a standard double room for one night, without breakfast, in peak season:
€€€€ over €200
€€€ €100–200
€€ €50–100
€ up to €50

Merlég Starlight Suiten Hotel

Mérleg utca 6; tel: 484-3700; www.starlighthotels.com; €€; M1: Vörösmarty tér, bus: 16, 105; map p.117 D1

Occupying a convenient location just behind the Four Seasons Gresham Palace, this apartment-style hotel (a branch of the dependable Starlight chain) offers smartly designed 'suites', each comprising a bedroom, lounge and bathroom.

BELVÁROS

Danubius Hotel Astoria

Kossuth Lajos utca 19–21; tel: 889-6000; www.danubius group.com; €€; M2: Astoria, tram: 47, bus: 7; map p.122 C3

First opened in 1914, the Astoria is an institution of a hotel built in the grand Empire style, and it is not surprising that the Nazis used it as their headquarters in Budapest during World War II. However, the sheen of luxury is now a little faded, though the Mirror Café and Restaurant – all velour and chandeliers – still gives a flavour of early 20th-century chic.

Hotel Anna

Gyulai Pál utca 14; tel: 327-2000; www.annahotel.hu; €–€€; M2: Blaha Lujza tér; map p.121 D4

This family-run budget hotel occupies a smart, yellow, double-fronted house not far from the National Museum. Inside, the 36 rooms – including one for guests with disabilities – are simple, yet have everything you could need, including an internet connection.

Hotel Zara

Só utca 6; tel: 577-0700; www.zarahotels.com; €€; M3: Kálvin tér, tram: 2, 47, 49; map p.122 B1

This 74-room four-star boutique hotel just off Váci utca (the city's main shopping street) is a fairly recent newcomer to Budapest. Clearly it has been a success as a much larger sister establishment, the Continental Hotel Zara, opened in summer 2010 in Dohány utca in the Jewish Quarter. Both hotels make clever use of colour coordination in their decor and combine style with comfort.

Inn-Side Hotel Kalvin House

Gönczy Pál utca 6; tel: 216-4365; www.kalvinhouse.hu; €€; M3: Kálvin tér, tram: 47, 49; map p.122 C1

With its handy location near the Liberty Bridge and the Market Hall, and spacious rooms, this small three-star hotel represents

Right: comfort and style at the Andrássy Hotel.

excellent value for money. The 30 rooms are simply but charmingly furnished with antiques, lending the hotel a reassuring old-world atmosphere.

New York Palace

Erzsébet körút 9–11; tel: 886-6111; www.boscolohotels.com; €€€€; M2: Blaha Lujza tér, tram: 4, 6; map p.121 E4

This is perhaps Budapest's most flamboyant and luxurious hotel. An architectural landmark, it was originally built as an insurance company's headquarters in the last years of the 19th century. It has recently been taken over by the Italian Boscolo chain of hotels and completely revamped, yielding 107 rooms of exuberant design and plush furnishings. Facilities include a spa, cigar bar, business centre and restaurant. SEE ALSO CAFÉS AND BARS, P.33; SPAS, P.106

OKTOGON TO HEROES' SQUARE

Andrássy Hotel

Munkácsy Mihály utca 5–7; tel: 462-2100; www.andrassyhotel.

com; €€€; M1: Bajza utca; map p.118 B3

This five-star boutique hotel occupies a 1930s Bauhaus-inspired building by Alfréd Hajós not far from Heroes' Square. There are 61 rooms and seven suites, some with four-poster beds. The in-house restaurant is the reputable **Baraka**, which ensures, at the very least, that breakfast is a pleasurable experience. The same chain of hotels also owns the Mamaison Residence Izabella just nearby (at Iza-

Left: boutique style at the Hotel Zara.

bella utca 61); this offers 38 suites, each with one to three bedrooms and a fully equipped kitchen. Guests at the Andrássy can also use the sauna and fitness centre of its sister hotel. SEE ALSO RESTAURANTS, P.98

Radio Inn
Benczúr utca 19; tel: 342-8347; www.radioinn.hu; €€; M1: Bajza utca; map p.118 B3
As the official guesthouse of the Hungarian National Radio, this simple sanctuary is often busy with visiting radio journalists. It offers 34 self-catering apartments with one to three bedrooms. This is a

good choice for families: the rooms are spacious yet inexpensive, the location is the peaceful embassy quarter next to City Park, and there is a garden for children to play in.

For those looking for accommodation in youth hostels, check out the **Hungarian Youth Hostel Association** website (www.miszsz.hu) for recommendations. Membership of the **Hostelling International** organisation (www.hihostels.com) will secure you discounts on rates.

61

Language

E ven the most linguistically confident of non-Hungarian speakers is likely to feel daunted when attempting to get by in Hungarian. A Finno-Ugric language – related to Finnish and Estonian among others – and with an alphabet of 44 characters, Hungarian is a notoriously difficult language to learn, and local people will not expect you to have mastered it before you visit. It goes without saying, however, that any efforts to acquire a few basics will be readily appreciated. The following list is a selection of useful words and phrases to get you started.

In Hungarian the stress in a word is always on the first syllable (with the exception of some adopted foreign words), and each letter is pronounced separately. (This includes adjacent vowels and double consonants within, rather than at the end of, a word – the latter are longer than single consonants.) The length of the vowel is indicated by an accent, with a double acute accent marking a longer vowel than a single one, and a short vowel having no accent at all. A vowel with an umlaut is also short. Note that a 't' is added to a noun when it becomes the object of a sentence.

VOWELS

a quite like **o** in n**o**t (British pronunciation)
á like **a** in f**a**ther
e a sound between **e** in y**e**s and **a** in h**a**t
é like **a** in s**a**y
i like **ee** in f**ee**t (short)
í like **ee** in s**ee** (long)
o quite like **aw** in s**aw** (British pronunciation), but shorter
ó like **o** in bl**o**w

ö like **ur** in pleas**ur**e
ő similar to **ö** but longer
u like **u** in p**u**ll (British pronunciation)
ú like **oo** in c**oo**l
ü like **u** in French t**u**
ű similar to **ü** but longer

CONSONANTS

b, d, f, h, m, n, v, x, z as in English
c like **ts** in ne**ts**
cs like **ch** in **ch**ap
g always as in **g**o
gy like **d** in **d**ew
j like **y** in **y**es
k as in si**ck**
l as in **l**eap
ly like **y** in **y**es
ny like **ni** in o**ni**on
p as in si**p**
r pronounced with the tip of the tongue, like Scottish **r**
s like **sh** in **sh**oot
sz like **s** in **s**o
t as in si**t**
ty like **tu** in **tu**be
zs like **s** in plea**s**ure

BASIC PHRASES

Hello *Szervusz/Szia* (informal)
Goodbye/Bye *Viszontlátásra/Viszlát*

Yes/No *Igen/Nem*
Please *Kérem*
Thank you *Köszönöm*
No thank you *Köszönöm nem*
Excuse me *Bocsánat*
Sorry *Elnézést*
Please speak slowly *Tessék lassabban beszélni*
I don't understand *Nem értem*
I don't speak Hungarian *Nem beszélek magyarul*
Do you speak English? *Beszél angolul?*
I am English/American *Angol/amerikai vagyok*
Can you help me? *Kérhetem a segítségét?*
My name is .. *A nevem ..*
Is there... here? *Van itt...?*
Where is...? *Hol van...?*
Who? *Ki?*
Why? *Miért?*
When? *Mikor?*
How? *Hogyan?*
Railway station *Pályaudvar*
Airport *Repülőter*
Ticket Office *Pénztár*
Entrance/exit *Bejárat/kijárat*
Push/pull *Tolni/húzni*
Left/right *Bal/job*
Straight on *Egyenesen*

Left: when eating out, the menu decoder below will help.

Market *Piac*
Pharmacy *Patika*
Post office *Postahivatal*
Supermarket *Ábécé/ABC*

EATING OUT

May I have the menu, please? *Kérek egy étlapot?*
I'd like... *Kérnék...*
Waiter/Waitress *Pincér/Kisasszony*
Bon appétit! *Jó étvágyat!*
I'm a vegetarian *Vegetáriánus vagyok*
Where are the toilets? *Hol van a WC?*
Gents/Ladies *Férfi/Női*
The bill, please *Számlát kérek*
Is service included? *Ebben a felszolgálás is benne van?*
Lamb *Bárány*
Veal *Borjú*
Pepper (seasoning) *Borsot*
Potatoes *Burgonya*
Sugar *Cukor*
Mushrooms *Gomba*
Fish *Hal*
Chips *Hasábburgonya*
Duck *Kacsa*
Bread *Kenyeret*
Salmon *Lazac*
Goose *Liba*
Beef *Marha*
Rabbit *Nyúl*
Pepper (vegetable) *Paprika*
Trout *Pisztráng*
Carp *Ponty*
Rice *Rizs*
Pork *Sertéshús*
Salt *Sót*
Venison *Szarvas*
Pasta *Tészta*
Butter *Vajat*
Wine *Bor* (**Red**: *Vörös bor*; **White**: *Fehér bor*)
Coffee *Kávé*
Sparkling wine *Pezsgő*
Beer *Sör*
Milk *Tej*
Water *Víz* (**Mineral water**: *Ásványvíz*)

NUMBERS

Zero *Nulla*
One *Egy*
Two *Kettő, két*
Three *Három*
Four *Négy*
Five *Öt*
Six *Hat*
Seven *Hét*
Eight *Nyolc*
Nine *Kilenc*
Ten *Tíz*
One hundred *Száz*
One thousand *Ezer*

DAYS OF THE WEEK

Monday *Hétfő*
Tuesday *Kedd*
Wednesday *Szerda*
Thursday *Csütörtök*

Below: knowing a few Hungarian phrases is helpful.

Friday *Péntek*
Saturday *Szombat*
Sunday *Vasárnap*

TIME

What time is it? *Hány óra van?*
It is 1 o'clock *Egy óra van*
It is 2 o'clock *Két óra van*
Now *Most*
Today *Ma*
Tomorrow *Holnap*
Yesterday *Tegnap*
Early morning *Reggel*
Mid/late morning *Délelőtt*
Afternoon *Délután*
Evening *Este*
Open/closed *Nyitva/zárva*

EMERGENCIES

Help! *Segítség!*
Stop! *Stop!*
Police *Rendőrség*
Doctor *Orvos*
Ambulance *Mentőautó*
Hospital *Kórház*

SHOPPING

How much is this? *Ez mennyibe kerül?*
I'm just looking *Csak körülnézek*
Do you accept credit cards? *Fizethetek kártyával?*

63

Literature and Theatre

Bookish types will find Budapest to be congenial territory. There is no shortage of bookshops: new ones are opening all the time, while some of the old ones still have the blue neon sign of the owl outside that denoted state ownership during the Communist era. The city also has more than its fair share of theatres, several of which stage English-language productions. There is plenty of opportunity, therefore, to indulge your literary pursuits and to discover a little more of Hungary's national literature.

AUTHORS

Hungarian literature started to evolve into part of a distinctive national culture from around the 1770s, the time of the Enlightenment in Hungary. The ascendancy of the secular, the awakening of a national consciousness and the 'progress' associated with industrialisation led to language reform and growth in the publishing industry and its readership.

Major writers of the period include language reformer, translator and critic **Ferenc Kazinczy** (1759–1831), poet and dramatist **Mihály Vörösmarty** (1800–55), poet **Sándor Petőfi** (1823–49) and poet and translator **János Arany** (1817–82). Later in the 19th century, prose fiction gained increasing popularity. Among the best-known novelists and short-story writers are **Mór Jókai** (1825–1904) and **Kálmán Mikszáth** (1847–1910).

In the early 20th century, among the finest writers were those associated with the literary journal, *Nyugat* ('West'). Founded in 1908, it published poetry and prose, and showed the clear influence of the naturalism and symbolism movements that had taken root elsewhere in Europe. Among the first generation of writers included in the journal were the poets **Endre Ady** (1877–1919), **Mihály Babits** (1883–1941) and **Árpád Tóth** (1886–1928), and the novelists **Gyula Krúdy** (1878–1933) and **Zsigmond Móricz** (1879–1942). Perhaps the best of the second generation were the poets **Lőrinc Szabó** (1900–57) and **Attila József** (1905–37). Other important writers of the 20th century include the playwright and novelist **Ferenc Molnár** (1878–1952), novelist **Frigyes Karinthy** (1887–1938), and, more recently, novelists **Magda Szabó** (1917–2007) and **Imre Kertész** (1929–).

The **Ervin Szabó Library** is the city's main public lending library (Szabó Ervin tér 1; tel: 411-5000; www.fszek.hu; M3 Kálvin tér). It occupies a grand palace originally built in 1887 for a family of wealthy industrialists, the Wenckheims. The council acquired it in 1926 and converted it for its present use. Fortunately, much of the original wood panelled interior has been retained, and readers can still sink into an old armchair and read a book by the light of the chandeliers overhead.

Above: Központi Antikvárium.

FURTHER READING

Batki, John (ed.) *Krúdy's Chronicles: Turn-of-the-Century Hungary in Gyula Krúdy's Journals* (2001)
Garton Ash, Timothy *We*

Left: the Ervin Szabó Library is located in an old palace.

Nagymező utca, off Andrássy út, is often referred to as 'Budapest's Broadway'. Among the theatres here are the **Thália** (Nos 22–4; tel: 331-0500; www. thalia.hu), which presents plays (usually in Hungarian), dance performances and musicals; the **Tivoli** (No. 8; tel: 351-6812; www.budapestikamaraszinhaz. hu), the Art Nouveau home of the Budapest Chamber Theatre; and the **Operetta Theatre** (No. 17; tel: 312-4866; www. operettszinhaz.hu).

the People: The Revolution of 89 Witnessed in Warsaw, Budapest, Berlin and Prague (1990)
Gundel, Károly Gundel's Hungarian Cookbook (various editions)
Liddell, Alex The Wines of Hungary (2003)
Molnár, Ferenc The Paul Street Boys (1927)
Pressburger, Giorgio and Nicola Homage to the Eighth District: Tales from Budapest (1990)

BOOKSHOPS
Alexandra
Andrássy út 39; tel: 484-8000; www.alexandra.hu; daily 10am–10pm; M1: Oktogon; map p.118 A2
As well as a large bookstore, these grand premises also house a smart café. Alexandra's antiquarian branch is a few doors down at No. 35 (tel: 486-1529).

Atlantisz
Király utca 2; tel: 267-6258; www.atlantiszkiado.hu; Mon–Fri 10am–6pm, Sat 10am–2pm; M1, 2, 3: Deák Ferenc tér; map p.122 B4

This is a good port of call for new books, including a selection of English-language titles.

Központi Antikvárium
Múzeum körút 13–15; tel: 317-3514; M2: Astoria, tram: 47, 49; map p.122 C2
Múzeum körút is lined with second-hand and antiquarian bookshops. This one is among the largest, stocking a wide variety of Hungarian (and some foreign-language) books and maps.

THEATRE
Given the difficulty of the Hungarian language, few visitors will feel up to sitting through a night of Hungarian theatre. However, there are a few theatres that do stage English-language productions.

Merlin International Theatre
Gerlóczy utca 4; tel: 317-9338; www.merlinszinhaz.hu; box office: daily 2–7pm; M1, 2, 3: Deák Ferenc tér; map p.122 B3
The Merlin presents regular English- and German-

language productions. Look out for shows put on by resident English-language company, Scallabouche.

National Theatre
Bajor Gizi Park 1; tel: 476-6868; www.nemzetiszinhaz. hu; box office open Mon–Fri 10am–6pm, Sat–Sun 2–6pm; HÉV: Lagymányosi-híd, tram: 2
Opened in 2002, the National presents classic theatre, from Sophocles to Stoppard. The majority of productions are in Hungarian, but there are also regular English-language shows by the Madhouse repertory company (www.madhousetheatre.hu), who also perform at the Merlin (see left).

Below: inside the Merlin.

Monuments

It seems that throughout Hungarian history, each time a new regime has come to power, it has erected its own monuments to promote its credo and suggest a sense of permanence. Ironically, regimes have come and gone time and again, and the number of monuments has multiplied, with obsolete statues being moved around, reassigned or parked where few go. Today, these relics merely give an indication of just how colourful yet traumatic Hungarian history has been. See also the *Architecture, p.26,* and *Communist-era Heritage, p.42* sections of this book for other interesting monuments.

CASTLE DISTRICT

Fishermen's Bastion (Halászbástya)

Szentháromság tér; daily 9am–9pm; admission charge for upper bastion; bus: 16; map p.116 B1

Located behind the Mátyás Church, the Fishermen's Bastion offers spectacular views of the river and Pest beyond. It was built in 1895 – in a strange hotchpotch of styles – by Frigyes Schulek, the same architect who was employed to revamp the Mátyás Church. The seven turrets symbolise the seven original Hungarian tribes. The reason for the name, however, is mysterious, though it may owe something to the fact that the defence of this part of the bastion was allocated to the fishermen's guild during the 18th century.

Labyrinth (Budavári Labirintus)

Úri utca 9; tel: 212-0207; www. labirintus.com; daily 9.30am–7.30pm; admission charge; bus: 16; map p.116 B1

Above: the atmospheric Fishermen's Bastion.

A doorway on Úri utca opens on to a staircase that takes you down into a subterranean network of tunnels and caves. Originally hollowed out by the natural springs that permeate the limestone bedrock, they have since been extended and linked up by man for accommodation, storage and, during World War II, shelter from bombs.

The labyrinth is now open to the public, who, by the light of oil lamps, are given guided tours of the 1,200m (4,000ft) of passageways and cellars.

Turul Bird

Szent György tér 2; funicular (sikló), bus: 16; map p.120 A4

As you alight from the funicular railway to the Castle District, you are confronted with the sculpture of a large bird perched beside the gateway to the Royal Palace and looking out over the city below. The Turul Bird is a mythical beast that is said to have raped the grandmother of Árpád, who was later to establish the first dynasty of Hungarian kings. When Árpád led the Magyar tribes in their conquest of the Carpathian basin

In the little square in the Castle District where Úri utca and Szentháromság utca meet, there is a bronze equestrian statue of András Hadik (1710–90), a distinguished Hussar who was a favourite of the Empress Maria Theresa. You will notice that the horse's testicles are very shiny. It is traditional for students to rub them for good luck before exams.

Left: the Turul Bird greets visitors to the Castle District.

Queen Elizabeth Statue (Erzsébet királyné-szobor)

Döbrentei tér; tram: 19, 41, bus: 7; map p.120 B3

In a small square by the Elizabeth Bridge is a seated statue that pays tribute to the pro-Hungarian wife of Emperor Franz Joseph. After the Compromise of 1867, by which Franz Joseph tried to appease Hungarian nationalism by creating the Dual Monarchy of Austria-Hungary, Elizabeth, now Queen of Hungary, developed increasing sympathy for the nation's causes. To the irritation of the court in Vienna (and her husband, with whom relations were strained), she spent much time in Budapest, learned Hungarian and was on close terms with the leading figures of the time, becoming lovers with several of them, including, reputedly, Count Andrássy.

Then, in 1898, while on a visit to Geneva, she was stabbed by an Italian anarchist and died shortly afterwards. There was a period of national mourning in Hungary, and a subscription was launched for a memorial. Eventually, after numerous competitions, a sculptor, György Zala, was commissioned and the result shows Elizabeth in the beauty of her youth with roses beside her. Originally, the statue was positioned in Március 15 tér at the other end of the bridge, but during the Communist era it was removed. It finally ended up here in 1986.

in 896, the Turul Bird flew with the invaders, carrying the sword of Attila the Hun.

The bronze sculpture you see today was executed by Gyula Donáth in 1905, just a few years after the one-thousandth anniversary of Árpád's greatest victory.

SEE ALSO PALACES AND HOUSES, P.88

SOUTH OF THE CASTLE DISTRICT: GELLÉRT HILL AND TABÁN

The Citadel (Citadella)

Gellért-hegy; tel: 466-5794; www.citadella.hu; tram: 18, bus: 27; map p.120 B2

After the Austrians had defeated the Hungarians in their uprising and subsequent War of Independence (1848–9), they reasserted their power in Budapest by building the Citadel. Between 1850 and 1854, forced Hungarian labour and even Hungarian architects slaved away on building this massive fortress and gun emplacement looking out over the city below. Thankfully, however, its

60 cannons were never used – though, in an ironic twist, the annual St Stephen's Day fireworks (20 August) are now launched from here by the Hungarian army.

When the Austrian garrison finally left in 1897, the Citadel was used as a prison, then a hostel for the homeless, until, in the 1960s, it was converted into a leisure complex. Today, there is a budget hotel, a café and an unfortunately uninspiring exhibition on the history of Gellért Hill.

SEE ALSO HOTELS, P.57

Below: historical pictures displayed at the Citadel.

In the square between the Fishermen's Bastion and the Mátyás Church is a statue of St Stephen, the king who converted Hungary into a Christian nation. The statue *(right)* was made by Alajos Stróbl for the celebration of the Magyar millennium in 1896 (the Magyars conquered the Carpathian Basin in AD896). The plinth, on the other hand, was designed by Frigyes Schulek, and includes sculpted reliefs showing events in the life of King Stephen.

St Gellért Statue

Gellért-hegy; tram: 18, bus: 27; map p.120 B3

On the side of Gellért Hill facing the city is a monument that marks the very spot where St Gellért was martyred in 1046. By background a Benedictine abbot, born in Venice in about AD980, Gellért came to Hungary to help convert the Magyars to Christianity and to tutor King Stephen's son, Imre. Following Stephen's death, however, those who sought to return to the old pagan religion struck out against the new Christian establishment. A mob attacked Gellért, tied him to a cart and pushed it off the cliff.

The monument commemorating the atrocity shows the saint holding a cross and a convert kneeling at his feet. Sculpted by Gyula Jankovits, it was erected in 1904.

NORTH OF THE CASTLE DISTRICT: VÍZIVÁROS, ROZSADOMB AND MARGARET ISLAND

Bodor Musical Well

Margitsziget; bus: 26

In the 1820s, an inventor called Péter Bodor created a hydraulically powered musical fountain in a town in what is now Romania. Unfortunately, only a few years later, in 1836, it was destroyed by a snow-storm. In 1936, a replica (this time powered by electricity) was built at the northern end of Margaret Island. To this day, it plays its chimes on the hour, while the gilded statue on top of the cupola rotates every 24 hours.

ÓBUDA

Military Town Amphitheatre

Nagyszombat utca 5; daily 24 hours; free; HÉV: Szépvölgyi út, bus: 86

In the 2nd century AD, the Romans built a large amphitheatre to enter-tain the legionaries and families who lived in the permanent camp nearby. Archaeologists believe that the structure could have accommodated up to 15,000 spectators to watch the gladiatorial contests.

LIPÓTVÁROS

Liberty Square (Szabadság tér)

M2: Kossuth Lajos tér, tram: 2, bus: 15; map p.117 D2

Apart from the obelisk and the nearby statue of Imre Nagy, there are a couple of other interesting monuments on Szabad-ság tér.

The first is a statue of Harry Hill Bandholtz, an American general who led a peacekeeping force in Budapest in 1919. He is credited with saving the National Museum from being looted by Roma-nian soldiers by securing the doors with what little he could lay his hands on – censorship seals. The mere sight of the American eagle is said to have made the marauding Romanians back off.

The second monu-ment is a plaque by the entrance to the American embassy at No. 12. This commemorates Cardinal Joseph Mindszenty, who resisted the Communist authorities' crackdown on religious expression in the early years after World War II. Having been imprisoned and tortured, he was released during the 1956 Uprising and sought asylum in the embassy. He lived here

for 15 years until, in 1971, the Vatican finally persuaded him to leave the country.
SEE ALSO COMMUNIST-ERA HERITAGE, P.43

BELVÁROS
Holocaust Memorial
Dohány utca 2; M2: Astoria, tram: 47, 49; map p.122 C3
In the courtyard behind the Great Synagogue (and also visible through the railings on Wesselényi utca) is the Holocaust Memorial. Made by sculptor Imre Varga in 1991, it takes the form of a silver willow tree, with each of its silver leaves inscribed with victims' names.
SEE ALSO CHURCHES, SYNAGOGUES AND SHRINES, P.41

OKTOGON TO HEROES' SQUARE
Heroes' Square (Hősök tere)
M1 Hősök tere; bus: 30, 105, trolleybus: 75, 79; map p.118 C4
Designed by György Zala and Albert Schikedanz in the 1890s, Heroes' Square was built to mark the Magyar millennium in 1896. The square's focal point is a column surmounted by the winged figure of the Archangel Gabriel, who, according to legend, appeared to King Stephen in a dream and ordered him to convert the pagan Magyars to Christianity in around AD1000. At the base of the column are statues of the chiefs of the seven Magyar tribes that conquered the Carpathian Basin in 896 and first established the nation on its current territory.

At the back of the square are two colonnades containing statues of famous leaders from Hungarian history. The statues of the Transylvanian nobles on the right-hand colonnade were added after World War II, replacing statues of Habsburg rulers who by then represented an undesirable Germanic past. On top of the colonnades are personifications of Work, Wealth, War, Peace, Knowledge and Glory.

VÁROSLIGET
Statue of Anonymous
Vajdahunyad Castle (Vajdahunyad Vára), Városliget; admission charge; M1: Széchenyi fürdő, bus: 30, 105, trolleybus: 75, 79; map p.119 C4
In the courtyard of Vajdahunyad Castle, facing the Agricultural Museum, is one of Hungary's most famous monuments. Miklós Ligeti's 1903 statue of an anonymous 12th-century chronicler of Hungarian history – his face obscured under a hood – is visited by thousands of superstitious Hungarians who hope that touching his pen will bring them good fortune.

On the south side of Vajdahunyad Castle in City Park is a statue of George Washington made by Gyula Bezerédi in 1906. Paid for by some of the 3 million Hungarians who had emigrated to the US by that time, it was the very first statue of the illustrious American to be erected in Europe. Nearby, in a corner niche around the back of the castle's Agriculture museum, is a bust of one of the most famous Hungarian-Americans, Béla Lugosi, better known as Count Dracula.

Above: the evocative Holocaust Memorial.

Below: Heroes' Square is still a big tourist draw.

Monuments

Museums and Galleries

As well as prestigious art galleries, and institutions that present the established view of the country's history, Budapest also possesses an extraordinary number of highly eccentric museums. Where else would you find collections devoted to the ambulance services, telephony or the chill-casting of iron? And if you are passionate about stained glass, criminology or stamps, then there are places here where you will feel at home. In addition to the museum listings below, see also *Communist-era Heritage, p.42*, and *Music, p.80*.

CASTLE DISTRICT

Budapest History Museum (Budapesti Történeti Múzeum)
Budavári Palota, E épület, Szent György tér 2; www.btm.hu; tel: 487-8887; mid-May–mid-Sept daily 10am–6pm, Mar-mid-May and mid-Sept–Oct Wed–Mon 10am–6pm, Nov–Feb Wed–Mon 10am–4pm; admission charge; bus: 16; map p.120 A4
Entrance to the History Museum is via the Lion Courtyard of the Royal Palace (behind the National Gallery). Starting on the lower ground floor, visitors can see vaulted rooms from the earlier palace of Sigismund of Luxembourg (reigned 1387–1437) as well as the hall of the later, Renaissance palace of King Mátyás (reigned 1458–90).

On the ground floor are the extraordinary Gothic statues of knights and their ladies and retainers, unearthed during archaeological digs in 1974. The first floor takes you from the expulsion of the Turks by the Habsburgs in 1686 right up to the city's *Belle Epoque* around 1900.

Finally, on the top floor, you are transported back to Hungary's formation, with treasures such as golden bridles and stirrups from burial mounds on the Pannonian Plain.

Hungarian National Gallery
Budavári Palota, A-B-C-D épület, Szent György tér 2; tel: 20 4397-325; www.mng.hu; Tue–Sun 10am–6pm; admission charge; bus: 16; map p.120 A4

Right: see great art at the Hungarian National Gallery.

Left: the Ernst Museum *(see p.74)* is also decorative outside.

Budapest's Best Museums

Art: Museum of Fine Arts *(p.78)*; Hungarian National Gallery *(p.70)*; Ludwig Museum of Contemporary Art *(p.76)*
History: Hungarian National Museum *(p.77)*; Budapest History Museum *(p.70)*; Aquincum Museum *(p.73)*
Science: Electrotechnology Museum *(p.76)*; Semmelweis Museum of Medical History *(p.72)*

Cubism) that were occurring elsewhere in Europe.
SEE ALSO PALACES AND HOUSES, P.88

Left: displays at the Budapest History Museum.

Occupying several wings of the Royal Palace, the National Gallery's main entrance faces the Danube, near to the statue of Prince Eugene of Savoy (1663–1736), who led the Christian armies that liberated Hungary from Turkish rule. The gallery is devoted to Hungarian art, and takes visitors chronologically from the Middle Ages on the ground floor to the 20th century on the third floor.

Highlights include the sculpted head of King Béla III (*c.*1200) and the sculptural masterpiece, the *Madonna and Child from Toporc* (*c.*1420) on the ground floor, while on the first floor there is the museum's definitive survey of 19th-century Hungarian painting. Famous pictures here include Mihály Munkácsy's *Yawning Apprentice* (1868) and Pál Szinyei Merse's *Picnic in May* (1873), a reworking of Manet's *Le Déjeuner sur l'Herbe* composition. The 20th-century art on the second and third floors is less distinctive, much of it deriving from artistic developments (such as Expressionism and

Museum of Military History (Hadtörténeti Múzeum)

Tóth Árpád sétány 40; tel: 325-1600; www.hm-him. hu; Tue–Sun, Apr–Sept 10am–6pm, Oct–Mar 10am–4pm; admission charge; bus: 16; map p.116 B2

Appropriately enough, this museum is housed in a former barracks, built in 1847, just in time for the Hungarian War of Independence. Inside, you can see all manner of military clobber, from the uniforms of Hussars to the tools in trade of the occupying army of Soviet

Russia – sniper rifles, border guards' binoculars and missile launchers.

Telephony Museum (Telefónia Múzeum)

Országház utca 30; tel: 201-8188; www.postamuzeum.hu; Tue–Sun 10am–4pm; admission charge; bus: 16; map p.116 B1

Hungary's principal contribution to the history of telephony was made by Tivadar Puskás, who invented the telephone exchange. His first hand-operated telephone exchange with crossbar switchboard (which still works) is the museum's prize exhibit.

SOUTH OF THE CASTLE DISTRICT: GELLÉRT HILL AND TABÁN

Semmelweis Museum of Medical History (Semmelweis Orvostörténeti Múzeum)

Apród utca 1-3; tel: 375-3533; www.semmelweis.museum.hu; admission charge; Tue–Sun, Mar–Oct 10.30am–5.30pm, Nov–Feb 10.30am–3.30pm; tram: 18, 19, bus: 5, 86; map p.120 B3

Ignác Semmelweis, the doctor famous for discovering the cause of puerperal (or childbirth)

Above: see old switchboards at the Telephony Museum.

fever, was born in this house in 1818. Often dismissed in his own time – despite saving thousands of lives – Semmelweis's achievements only received widespread recognition following Louis Pasteur's work on germ theory. Indeed, nowadays, the act of rejecting a new discovery without due consideration is known as the Semmelweis Reflex.

Inside the museum, Semmelweis's surgery has been preserved with its original furnishings. There is also a reconstruction of the Holy Ghost Pharmacy, which was established in Pest in 1786. The display

For an insight into life in the Castle District in the 18th century, visit the **Golden Eagle Pharmacy Museum** (Arany Sas Patikamúzeum; Tárnok utca 18; tel: 375-9772; www.semmelweis.museum.hu; 15 Mar–31 Oct Tue–Sun 10.30am–5.30pm; 1 Nov–14 Mar Tue–Thur 10.30am–3.30pm, Fri–Sun 10.30am–5.30pm; admission charge; bus: 16). Trading under the name 'Golden Eagle' from 1740, the original pharmacy business was actually more alchemist's than apothecary's, as you can see from the reconstructed laboratory in one of the rooms (complete with furnace, crucibles, jars of minerals and pestles and mortars). Elsewhere in the museum are examples of old prescriptions written out to people and also animals, as well as dusty tomes on medicine by Hippocrates, Avicenna and Paracelsus. Visitors should not leave without seeing the glass cabinet containing a 2,000-year-old mummified head. It was used as the source of 'mummy head dust' – believed to cure bronchitis.

of skulls, mummies, a shrunken head and pictures of antiquated treatments is not for the squeamish.

NORTH OF THE CASTLE DISTRICT: VÍZIVÁROS, ROZSADOMB AND MARGARET ISLAND

Foundry Museum (Öntödei Múzeum)

Bem József utca 20; tel: 201-4370; www.omm.hu/ontode; Tue–Sun 9am–5pm; admission charge; tram: 4, 6, bus: 86; map p.116 C3

Left: excavated Roman ruins at the Aquincum site.

Right: a Roman bathing complex at the Bath Museum.

Perhaps unsurprisingly, this is the only foundry in Central Europe preserved as a tourist attraction. It actually, however, played an important role in the development of the country, facilitating the laying of the country's vast railway network in the second half of the 19th century. The foundry was built between 1858 and 1862 by Ábrahám Ganz, who had patented a number of industrial applications that enabled him to chill-cast iron railway wheels, railway-crossing points and a range of other useful products. Remarkably, the foundry continued operating according to the same industrial processes until 1964.

ÓBUDA
Aquincum Museum
Szentendrei út 135; tel: 250-1650; www.btm.hu; Tue–Sun, May–Sept 10am–6pm, 15–30 Apr and Oct 10am–5pm; admission charge; HÉV: Aquincum
Aquincum (literally 'abundant in water') was the name of the Roman town that was founded here in 35BC. Over the next four centuries, the town's population grew to 40,000, and all the usual Roman facilities – baths, temples and amphitheatres – were built to cater for them. Much of the town was excavated in the 19th century, and a museum was built to exhibit the finds. There are statues, sarcophagi, mosaics, jewellery, and an extraordinary water-powered organ (which has

been reconstructed so that it can be played).

Bath Museum – Thermae Maiores
Flórián tér 3-5 (pedestrian underpass); tel: 250-1650; www.btm.hu; Tue–Sun May–Sept 10am–6pm, 15–30 Apr and Oct 10am–5pm, Nov–14 Apr depending on weather; free; HÉV: Árpád híd, tram: 1, bus: 6, 86
The area around Flórián tér was once the site of the Roman military town that accommodated a legion of some 6,000 soldiers. The remains of the town's bathing complex can be seen in a sectioned-off area under the large dual-carriageway flyover.

Hercules Villa
Meggyfa utca 19-21; tel: 250-1650; www.btm.hu; mid-Apr–Oct: group visits only (arrange by phone); free; bus: 6, 86 (Bogdáni út stop)
The quality of the mosaics that have survived at what was once a 12-room villa suggests that the Roman family who lived here must have been very wealthy indeed. The mosaics,

several of which illustrate the Hercules myths, were probably imported ready-made from Italy. One of the best examples has now been transferred to the Aquincum museum, but several fine mosaics remain *in situ*.

Imre Varga Collection
Laktanya utca 7; tel: 250-0274; Tue–Sun 10am–6pm; admission charge; HÉV: Árpád híd, tram: 1
Imre Varga (1923–) is one of Hungary's most famous contemporary sculptors. Among his most notable public monuments is the memorial to Imre Nagy. Another of his pieces, *People Waiting*, can be seen in the small square at the end of Laktanya utca. This gallery (and the garden behind) exhibits a representative selection of the prolific artist's work.
SEE ALSO MONUMENTS, P.69

Kassák Memorial Museum
Fő tér 1; tel: 368-7021; Tue–Sun 10am–5pm; admission charge; HÉV: Árpád híd, tram: 1
Located within the east

Right: traditional textiles at the Zsigmond Kun Folk Art Collection.

wing of the Zichy Palace, this museum commemorates the life and work of Lajos Kassák (1887–1967), an artist, poet and critic of the modernist avant-garde. The exhibition consists of paintings, photographs, manuscripts and books.

Kiscelli Museum
Kiscelli utca 108; tel: 388-8560; www.btm.hu; Apr–Oct 10am–6pm, Nov–Mar 10am–4pm; admission charge; tram: 17, bus: 60, 165
To the east of Óbuda, on Mátyás Hill, is a former monastery built by the aristocratic Zíchy family in the mid-18th century. Today the building is home to Budapest's municipal art collection, which comprises mostly Hungarian paintings and sculptures, from the 19th and 20th centuries. There is also a ruined church (bombed during World War II) as well as fine gardens.

Textile and Clothing Industry Museum
Lajos utca 136–8; tel: 430-1387; www.textilmuzeum.hu; Tue–Thur 10am–4pm, Fri 10am–2pm; admission charge; HÉV: Árpád híd, tram: 1
The Goldberger family established an indigo-printing workshop in this building in 1784, and the family firm continued and expanded until its last scion, Leo Goldberger, died in a concentration camp in 1945. The museum today preserves textile printing, knitting, sewing and spinning machines from the last 200 years, along with examples of the sorts of things such machines produced.

Vasarely Museum
Szentlélek tér 6; tel: 388-7551; www.vasarely.tvn.hu; Tue–Sun 10am–5.30pm; admission charge; HÉV: Árpád híd, tram: 1
The Hungarian-born painter Victor Vasarely (1906–97) was one of the pioneers of the Op Art movement, which used optical illusions to explore the relationship between seeing two-dimensional images and interpreting them. This gallery, in part of the Zichy Palace, exhibits a survey of his work.

Zsigmond Kun Folk Art Collection
Fő tér 1; tel: 250-1020; www.museum.hu/budapest/kunzsigmond; Tue–Fri 2–6pm, Sat–Sun 10am–6pm; admission charge; HÉV: Árpád híd, tram: 1, bus: 86
The core of this museum is the collection of Zsigmond Kun (1893–2000). The exhibition sets out the painted village furniture, textiles and pottery that he and his wife lived with for decades.

LIPÓTVÁROS
Ernst Museum
Nagymező utca 8; tel: 413-1310; www.mucsarnok.hu; Tue–Sun 11am–7pm; admission charge; M1: Opera, bus: 105; map p.118 A1
Administered from the Palace of Art (Műcsarnok) in Heroes' Square *(see*

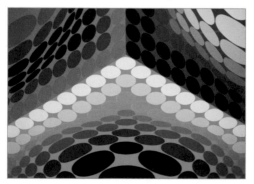

Left: Op Art on display at the Vasarely Museum.

Left: folk culture is explored at the Ethnographical Museum.

p.79), the Ernst Museum is another of the city's venues for temporary exhibitions of contemporary art.

Ethnographical Museum (Néprajzi Múzeum)

Kossuth Lajos tér 12; tel: 473-2400; www.neprajz. hu; Tue–Sun 10am–6pm; admission charge; M2: Kossuth Lajos tér, tram: 2, bus: 15; map p.117 D2

The city's folk museum is housed within the former Supreme Court building. You enter via the cavernous entrance hall, which was once used as a stand-in for Buenos Aires in the film version of *Evita*. The museum's collections are displayed upstairs, organised according to the themes of childhood, marriage, religion, agriculture and so on. Exhibits such as folk costumes, painted furniture, ceramics and even village shop fronts are accompanied by vintage photographs that put the items into context.

House of Hungarian Art Nouveau

Honvéd utca 3; tel: 269-4622; www.magyarszecessziohaza. hu; Tue–Sat 10am–5pm; admission charge; M2: Kossuth Lajos tér, bus: 115; map p.117 D2

This beautifully restored Art Nouveau building is home to a privately owned museum of furniture, ceramics, glassware and other applied arts in the Art Nouveau style. There is also a pleasant café.

Hungarian House of Photography

Nagymező utca 20; tel: 473-2666; www.maimano.hu; Mon–Fri 2–7pm, Sat–Sun 11am–7pm; admission charge; M1: Opera, bus: 105; map p.117 E2

This eccentric building in the theatre district was built for the photographer Manó Mai in 1894. It features paintings representing the six mythical 'muses of photography' and even a little cherub with a camera (between the ground and first floors). The various galleries and halls are used for temporary exhibitions of important photographers of the past and present. The József Pécsi Library of Photography on the third floor contains photo albums, books on photography and an archive.

Museum of the Ambulance Services

Markó utca 22; tel: 3744-008; www.mentok.hu; Mon–Fri 8am–4pm, Sat 8am–2pm; admission charge; M2: Kossuth tér, tram: 2; map p.117 E3

A symbol of civic pride, the city's ambulance service was first made the subject of an exhibition as part of the celebration of the Magyar Millennium in 1896. Today's museum has evolved from that time to incorporate vintage ambulances, antique medical equipment and a collection of photographs and other memorabilia.

Museum of the Hungarian Post Office

Andrássy út 3; tel: 269-6838; www.postamuzeum.hu; Tue–

Bookish types will enjoy the **Petőfi Literary Museum** (Károlyi Mihály utca 16; tel: 317-3611; www.pim.hu; Mon–Thur 10am–3pm; admission charge). Housed within the Károlyi Palace, Hungary's national museum of literature centres around an exhibition of the personal possessions and manuscripts of the poet Sándor Petőfi. Petőfi is considered a national hero for having sparked off the Hungarian War of Independence in 1848 by reciting his poem, 'National Song', from the steps of the National Museum *(see p.77)*. Other important holdings within the museum include a library of early editions of Hungarian works of literature, an archive of manuscripts, a photographic collection (including work by André Kertész), and a large assortment of the personal belongings of writers such as Gyula Krúdy, Endre Ady, Zsigmond Móricz and Mihály Babits (including swimsuits, musical instruments and kitchen utensils). The museum's sizeable collection of art includes paintings by Munkácsy, Rippl-Rónai and Zichy.

The **Ludwig Museum of Contemporary Art** can be found on the banks of the Danube to the south of the Belváros in the huge arts complex that also contains the **National Concert Hall** (Palace of Arts – Művészetek Palotája; Komor Marcell utca 1; tel: 555-3444; www.ludwigmuseum.hu; Tue–Sun 10am–8pm; admission charge; HÉV: Lágymányosi híd, tram: 2). The permanent exhibition on the third floor charts the history of modern art by placing Hungarian works in the context of paintings and sculptures by foreign artists such as Baselitz, Jasper Johns, Picasso and Warhol. The first and second floors are given over to temporary exhibitions of modern and contemporary art.

Sun 10am–6pm; admission charge; M1: Bajcsy-Zsilinszky út, bus: 105; map p.122 B4
The grand interiors of a palatial building on Andrássy út play host to this exhibition on Hungary's postal service. The collection of postboxes, post office furnishings, franking machines and other equipment is brought to life with a staff of mannequins dressed in old post-office uniforms.

Museum of Trade and Tourism
Szent István tér 15; tel: 375-6249; www.mkvm.hu; Wed–Mon 11am–7pm; admission charge; M1: Bajcsy-Zsilinszky út; map p.117 E1
Having in recent years relocated to a building near St Stephen's Basilica, this museum has not yet set up a permanent exhibition for its large collection of post-

ers, paintings, photographs, advertising material and commercial packaging. The temporary exhibitions are, however, well worth seeing. Recent ones have examined subjects as diverse as the life and work of chef Károly Gundel, Austrian typography, Easter eggs and Budapest café culture.

Underground Railway Museum (Földalatti Múzeum)
Deák Ferenc tér metro station; tel: 235-0207; www.bkv.hu/english/muzeum; Tue–Sun 10am–5pm; admission charge; M1, 2, 3: Deák Ferenc tér; map p.122 B4
A redundant tunnel within the city's largest metro station accommodates a collection of old underground trains and carriages.

BELVÁROS
Bible Museum
Ráday utca 28; tel: 217-6321; Tue–Sun 10am–5pm; free; M3: Kálvin tér, bus: 15; map p.121 D2
The history of the Bible is charted in an exhibition that includes handwritten and printed versions in a variety of languages. Highlights include the first complete Hungarian trans-

Above: the Electrotechnology Museum demonstrates scientific experiments.

lation and the first printed Greek New Testament issued by Erasmus.

Electrotechnology Museum (Magyar Elektrotechnikai Múzeum)
Kazinczy utca 21; tel: 342-5750; www.emuzeum.hu/hu; Mon–Fri 10am–5pm, Sat 9am–4pm; admission charge; M2: Astoria, tram: 4, 6, trolleybus: 74; map p.121 D4
Housed in a former electricity substation, the Electrotechnology Museum explains the rudiments of electricity production by

Right: the grand Hungarian National Museum.

Right: the Ludwig Museum of Contemporary Art.

re-creating famous experiments and demonstrating the workings of early generators and motors.

Hungarian National Museum (Magyar Nemzeti Múzeum)

Múzeum körút 14–16; tel: 338-2122; www.mnm.hu; Tue–Sun 10am–6pm; admission charge; M3: Kálvin tér, M2: Astoria, tram: 47, 49, bus: 9, 15, 7, 78; map p.121 D3

Hungary's largest museum charts the history of the nation from its earliest beginnings. Highlights include gold jewellery made by the Avars, who occupied the Hungarian Plains from AD567 to 804, St Stephen's coronation mantle, the 13th-century gold crown of Stephen V (brother of St Margaret) found in his grave on Margaret Island, the childhood armour of King Sigismund II of Poland and a fitted Baroque library. From more recent times there is a collection of memorabilia from the heyday of Hungarian cinema, and plenty of Communist-era propaganda posters.

Jewish Museum (Zsidó Múzeum)

Dohány utca 2; tel: 344-5409; www.zsidomuzeum.hu; May–Nov Mon–Thur 10am–6pm, Fri 10am–4pm, Nov–Apr Mon–Thur 10am–4pm, Fri 10am–2pm; admission charge; M2: Astoria, tram: 47, 49, bus: 7, 78, trolleybus 74; map p.122 C3

Located behind the Great Synagogue in the Jewish Quarter, this museum was built on the site of the birthplace of Theodor Herzl (1860–1904), founder of the Zionist movement. The exhibits inside include a 19th-century tapestry with the words of the Torah embroidered in miniature. It was used for covert worship during World War II. There are also plenty of photographs relating to the Holocaust in Hungary, where approximately 600,000 Jewish people were sent to the gas chambers in the months after the Nazis invaded in March 1944.

Outside, you can still see a section of the ghetto wall, erected in 1944. At that time, about 20,000 Jewish people took refuge in the synagogue. Tragically, the severe winter that followed killed some 7,000 of them; many were buried in the courtyard here, where Imre Varga's willow-tree memorial now stands.

SEE ALSO CHURCHES, SYNAGOGUES AND SHRINES, P.41; MONUMENTS, P.69

Museum of Applied Arts (Iparművészeti Múzeum)

Üllői út 33–37; tel: 456-5107; www.imm.hu; Tue–Sun 10am–6pm; admission charge; M3: Ferenc körút, tram: 4, 6; map p.121 D2

The spectacular building that houses this museum was designed by Ödön Lechner and Gyula Pártos in full-blown Secessionist style. The design incorporates folk-art motifs, makes liberal use of coloured pyrogranite tiles, and betrays more than a hint of Anglo-Indian styling.

The collection itself was formed to emulate the Victoria and Albert Museum in London and Vienna's Museum of Applied Arts. It embraces furniture, ceramics, glassware, textiles and metalwork. The permanent exhibition on the first floor includes the astronomical clock (1566) that belonged to Holy Roman Emperor Maximilian II, a musical automaton of a saint (1570), 17th-century dresses from the aristocratic Esterhazy family, as well as Zsolnay vases, Tiffany glassware, Lalique jewellery and Art Nouveau furniture.

OKTOGON TO HEROES' SQUARE

Ferenc Hopp Museum of Far Eastern Art (Kelet-Ázsiai Művészeti Múzeum)

Andrássy út 103; tel: 322-8476; www.hoppmuzeum.hu; Tue–Sun 10am–6pm; admission charge; M1: Bajza utca; map p.118 B3

The former home of Ferenc Hopp (1833–1919), optician and businessman, traveller and collector of Asian art, provides an extraordinary insight into the various cultures of the Orient. The thousands of objects on display provide a showcase of Chinese, Japanese, Korean, Indian, Tibetan and Mongolian art.

Geological Museum

Stefánia út 14; tel: 251-0999; www.mafi.hu; Thur, Sat–Sun 10am–4pm; admission charge; trolleybus: 74

Housed in a fine building by Ödön Lechner, Hungary's Geological Institute has created a charmingly old-fashioned exhibition of fossils, minerals and maps that takes you back to the pioneering days of the study of geology.

György Ráth Museum of Asiatic Art

Városligeti fasor 12; tel: 342-3916; www.hoppmuzeum. hu; Tue–Sun 10am–6pm; admission charge; M1: Bajza utca; map p.118 B2

As well as being the first director of the city's Museum of Applied Arts, György Ráth was also an important collector of art in his own right. This beautifully proportioned villa designed by Miklós Ybl was his home, and contains the vast array of Far Eastern artworks he amassed.

Miksa Róth Memorial House

Nefelejcs utca 26; tel: 341-6789; www.rothmuzeum.hu; Tue–Sun 2–6pm; admission charge; M1: Bajza utca, trolleybus: 70, 74; map p.118 C2

During this lifetime, Miksa Róth (1865–1944) achieved an international reputation as an artist of stained glass and mosaic. This museum has been established in what was his home and workshop from 1910 until his death. As well as examples of his art, visitors can see his furniture, carpets and collection of antiquities.

Museum of Criminology and Police History (Bűnügyi Múzeumot)

Mosonyi utca 7; tel: 477-2183; www.policehistorymus.com; Tue–Sun 9am–5pm; M2: Baross tér; map p.119 C1

From the glamorous to the macabre to the mundane, this museum's exhibits encompass notorious murders, Hungarian writers of detective fiction, police weapons and even stuffed police dogs.

Museum of Fine Arts (Szépművészeti Múzeum)

Dózsa György út 41; tel: 469-7100; www.mfab.hu; Tue–Sun 10am–5.30pm, Thur temporary exhibitions until 10pm; admission charge; M1: Hősök tere, bus: 30, 105, trolleybus: 75, 79; map p.118 B4

Hungary's premier art collection spans the history of art from the Ancient Egyptians to the 20th century. There are Egyptian mummies and sarcophagi, Greek sculptures, an impressive array of Old Masters (from Raphael to Velázquez), and a fair representation of 19th-century French art, including works by Courbet, Monet and Gauguin. The 20th-century collection is centred around Austrian and German painting; a

Below: the modern design of the Palace of Art.

Above: the Agricultural Museum is housed in a fantastical 19th-century castle.

wider survey of modern art can be seen at the Ludwig Museum of Contemporary Art *(see p.76)*.

Museum of Firefighting (Tűzoltó Múzeum)
Martinovics tér 12; tel: 261-3586; www.katasztrofavedelem.hu/muzeum; Tue–Sat 9am–4pm, Sat 9am–1pm; admission charge; bus: 28
Established in 1955, this museum is a repository of bygone firefighting paraphernalia, as well as records and relics from some of the more impressive conflagrations in the city's history.

Palace of Art (Műcsarnok)
Dózsa György út 37; tel: 460-7000; www.mucsarnok.hu; Tue–Wed and Fri–Sun 10am–6pm; Thur noon–8pm; admission charge; M1: Hősök tere, bus: 30, 105; map p.118 C4
The Palace of Art is the city's main venue for large-scale temporary exhibitions of art, many of which are shows touring from overseas.

Stamp Museum
Hársfa utca 47; tel: 341-5526; www.belyegmuzeum.hu; Tue–Sun 10am–6pm; admission charge; M2: Blaha Lujza tér, trolleybusi: 74; map p.118 B1
This museum, with its collection of 13 million stamps, should keep avid philatelists off the streets for a few hours.

VÁROSLIGET
Agricultural Museum
Vajdahunyad Vára, Városliget; tel: 363-1117; www.mmgm.hu; Tue–Sun 10am–5pm; admission charge; M1: Széchenyi fürdő, bus: 30, 105, trolleybus: 75, 79; map p.119 C4
Located within the fantasy castle built as part of the Magyar Millennium exhibition at the end of the 19th century, the Agricultural Museum has displays on horse, cattle and sheep breeding, and on hunting, fishing and winemaking. Exhibits include hunting trophies, stuffed animals and farm machinery.

Transport Museum (Közlekedési Múzeum)
Városligeti körút 11; tel: 273-3840; www.km.iif.hu; Tue–Fri 10am–5pm, Sat–Sun 10am–6pm (closes an hour earlier in winter); admission charge; tram: 1, trolleybus: 70, 72, 74; map p.119 D4
If you have an enthusiasm for steam trains, old trams, vintage cars and motorcycles, then this is the place to come. Nearby, on the same side of City Park, in a separate building, there is also a collection of light aircraft, an old helicopter and exhibits related to space exploration (Petőfi Csarnok, Zichy Mihály út 14; tel: 363-0809; May–mid-Oct Tue–Sun 10am–5pm; admission charge).

Many visitors to Budapest will find it worth their while to purchase a Budapest Card (www.budapestinfo.hu/en/budapest_card). This entitles the holder to discounts or free admission to most of the city's museums as well as free travel on all public transport. Cards can be bought for either 48- or 72-hour periods. They are sold at tourist information offices, in many hotels, at the larger metro stations and at many travel agencies.

Music

Budapest has an impressive musical heritage. A roll-call of great composers, from Haydn to Liszt to Bartók, has had close associations with the city. There are numerous concert halls, many as sumptuously decorated as palaces, and one of the finest 19th-century opera houses in Europe. And there is plenty for musical tastes that extend beyond classical – from grunge rock to operetta, from Hungarian folk to acid jazz. In addition to those listed below, for other musical venues in Budapest, see *Cafés and Bars, p.30*, and *Nightlife, p.84*. For more on music events, see *Festivals, p.46*.

MUSEUMS

Béla Bartók Memorial House (Bartók Béla Emlékház)
Csalán út 29; tel: 394-2100; www.bartokmuseum.hu; Tue–Sun 10am–5pm; admission charge; bus: 5, 29

On a leafy avenue in genteel Rozsadomb – a bus ride from Moszkva tér to Pasaréti tér – is the house

Jazz-lovers will find a lively scene in Budapest. The **Budapest Jazz Klub** (Múzeum utca 7; tel: 267-2610; www. bjc.hu) near the National Museum has live music every night, and entry to after-11pm jam sessions free of charge. Wednesday evenings usually feature folk ensembles. Nearby, the **Jazz Garden** (Veres Pálné utca 44A; tel: 266-7364; www.jazzgarden.hu) puts on concerts daily at 8.30pm in its cosy cellar premises. The **New Orleans** just off Nagymező utca (Lovag utca 5; tel: 269-4951; www.neworleans.hu) is a plusher venue offering jazz gigs in addition to party nights and stand-up comedy.

of the composer Béla Bartók (1881–1945). This fine suburban villa is now a museum and an 80-seat venue for chamber concerts (often using one of Bartók's pianos). One floor of the house preserves the composer's living rooms and study – with his collection of folk art, painted furniture, pottery and textiles, and his Edison cylinder machine for recording folk songs in the field. The top floor displays his other possessions in glass cabinets. There are his binders of pressed flowers, trays of beetles, folk costumes, musical instruments and his pocket metronome.

Franz Liszt Memorial Museum (Liszt Ferenc Emlékmúzeum)
Vörösmarty utca 35; tel: 322-9804; www.lisztmuseum. hu; Mon–Fri 10am–6pm, Sat 9am–5pm, closed 1–20 Aug; admission charge; M1: Oktogon; map p.118 A2

The large building on the corner of Andrássy út and Vörösmarty utca used

Above: the Béla Bartók Memorial House.

to function as Hungary's Academy of Music (Zeneakadémia) before the new Academy building opened on Liszt Ferenc tér. The Academy's first president was the virtuoso pianist and composer Franz Liszt. His flat on the first floor is preserved as a museum.

As well as his pianos, the flat is packed with mementoes of his extraordinary life. There is his prie-dieu, crucifix and rosaries (he was a novice for the priesthood and wore clerical vestments), and pictures of several of

Left: Sziget is Hungary's largest rock festival *(see p.83)*.

of writing, the building in which the museum is situated was closed for renovation until further notice.

CONCERT VENUES
Budapest
Congress Centre
Jagelló út 1–3; tel: 372-5400; www.bcc.hu; box office open Wed, Fri 4–6.30pm, Sat 10am–1pm; M2: Déli pu, then tram: 61

Located on the Buda side of the river, this soulless conference centre has a 2,000–capacity auditorium that is often used for concerts, particularly when they need to pack in the punters to pay for international performers.

Duna Palace
Zrínyi utca 5; tel: 317-2754; www.bm.hu/dunapalota; box office open daily 8–11pm; M1: Vörösmarty tér, tram: 2; map p.117 D1

This grand neo-Baroque concert hall is home to the Danubia Szimfonikus Zenekar, a young orchestra that performs a programme of classical lollipops. In the summer, the venue also hosts a series of folk dancing shows by the Duna Folk Ensemble.

his lovers, for he was also a notorious womaniser and fathered numerous illegitimate children. There is also his silver conducting baton, his cigars and snuff box, his card table and all kinds of honours and gifts given by the great and good.

Museum of Musical History
Táncsics Mihály út 7; tel: 214-6770; www.zti.hu/museum; Tue–Sun 10am–4pm; admission charge; bus: 16; map p.116 B2

The magnificent Baroque Erdődy-Hatvany Palace in the Castle District is home to Budapest's music museum as well as the Bartók archives. There is also a concert hall, and the regular recitals are often accompanied by guided tours of the building (check the website for details). The museum puts on exhibitions on the great composers and musical history of Hungary.

Right: in the Franz Liszt Memorial Museum.

Zoltán Kodály Memorial Museum (Kodály Zoltán Emlékmúzeum)
Andrássy út 89; tel: 352-7106; www.kodaly-inst.hu; closed until further notice; M1: Kodály körönd; map p.118 B3

This, the home of Zoltán Kodály (1882–1967), has been preserved exactly as the composer left it on his death. Here are his pianos, cello, extensive library, collection of folk ceramics and embroideries, and photographs and other keepsakes of famous musical friends. There is also a large archive. Unfortunately, at the time

Above: an outdoor concert in Városliget.

Palace of Arts (Művészetek Palotája)
Komor Marcell utca 1; tel: 555-3300; www.mupa.hu; box office open daily 10am–6pm or until end of performance; HÉV: Lagymányosi-híd, tram: 2
The Palace of Arts complex opened in 2005, and houses the Béla Bartók National Concert Hall, the Festival Theatre, the Ludwig Museum of Contemporary Art and a number of smaller halls and auditoria. The acoustically excellent Bartók Hall is the place in Budapest to see the big names on the international classical music circuit. The other halls in the complex

host children's concerts and workshops, jazz and world music performances, and dance and theatre productions.
SEE ALSO MUSEUMS AND GALLERIES, P.76

Vigadó
Vigadó tér 1; tel: 318-9903; www.vigado.hu; box office opens one hour before performances; M1: Vörösmarty tér; map p.122 A3
The Vigadó (the name means 'place for merriment') was originally built in 1865 to designs by Frigyes Feszl. It has recently been renovated and, pristine and white, looks as if it is made out of cake icing. Inside, there is a 700-seat concert hall and a 220-seat chamber music venue. The programme consists mainly of popular classics and dance performances by the Hungarian State Folk Ensemble.

Zeneakadémia
Liszt Ferenc tér 8; tel: 342-0179; www.zeneakademia.hu; box office: Mon–Fri 10am–8pm, Sat–Sun 2–8pm, closed July–Aug; M1: Oktogon; map p.118 A1
The home of the Franz Liszt Academy of Music

> Located near to the State Opera and the Liszt Academy of Music, **Liszt Ferenc Zeneműbolt** (Andrássy út 45; tel: 322-4091) is a useful shop for sheet music, CDs and books on music.

is one of the most extravagant Seccessionist buildings in Budapest. Designed by Flóris Korb and Kálmán Giergl, and completed in 1907, its facade features a heroic statue of composer Franz Liszt by Alajos Stróbl, together with six sculpted reliefs by Ede Telcs of the stages in the development of music. Inside, every surface seems to be either gilded, wood-panelled or richly decorated.

The main concert hall has a wonderful fresco, *Hungarian Wedding Procession in the 14th century* (1907) by Aladár Körösfői Kriesch. The hall is also renowned for its outstanding acoustics.

OPERA
Budapest Operetta Theatre (Budapesti Operettsház)
Nagymező utca 17; tel: 353-2172; www.operettszinhaz.hu; box office: Mon–Fri 10am–2.30pm and 3–7pm, Sat–Sun 1–7pm; M1: Opera; map p.118 A2
Just around the corner from the State Opera, on Budapest's 'Broadway', is this pretty theatre – all stucco, gilding and red velvet – built by Viennese architects Fellner and Helmer in 1894. The programme consists of light opera and musicals.

Left: the Seccessionist Zeneakadémia.

Music

Right: crowds arrive at the Budapest Operetta Theatre.

Hungarian State Opera House (Magyar Állami Operaház)

Andrássy út 22; box office tel: 353-0170; www.opera. hu; box office: Mon–Sat 11am–5pm or the beginning of a performance; M1: Opera; map p.117 E1

Budapest has one of the finest 19th-century opera houses in Europe, with lavish interiors, excellent acoustics and even air conditioning. When it was opened, in 1884, however, the Emperor Franz Joseph was less than pleased. He had largely paid for it, stipulating that it should be smaller than Vienna's, but was now peeved that, although smaller, it was also prettier and more opulent.

The building has been lucky enough to survive

two world wars almost unscathed, and renovations during the 1980s – including renewal of the gilding with 300,000 pieces of gold leaf – have kept it looking as sumptuous and vibrant as when the original architect, Miklós Ybl, had originally built it. Inside, the frescoes of the nine muses in the lobby and the ceiling

painting of Mount Olympus in the auditorium are particularly fine.

Today, visitors can take a guided tour of the building (daily at 3pm and 4pm in various languages), as well as attend performances of the state opera company and the Hungarian National Ballet. Tickets are very reasonably priced.

Most large-scale rock and pop concerts in Budapest are held at the **Budapest Arena** *(see Sports, p.111)* or the **Petőfi Csarnok** in City Park (Zichy Mihály út 14; tel: 363-3730; www.petoficsarnok.hu). For more intimate gigs try **A38**, **Filter Klub** or **Gödör Klub** *(see Nightlife, p.84 and 86).* Another important venue, with a high-quality line-up, and sound and light systems to match, is **Wigwam Rock Club**, located in the south of Buda (Fehérvári út 202; tel: 208-5569; www.wigwamrockclub. hu; tram: 41, 47). By far the biggest attraction for rock fans, however, is the **Sziget Festival** in August each year *(see Festivals, p.47).* Big-name acts from around the world and a host of local bands descend on Óbuda Island to keep music live.

Below: opulent frescoes at the Hungarian State Opera House.

Nightlife

Budapest's nightlife may not be the throbbing hub of European style or a magnet for the top international DJs, but it more than makes up for its lack of profile with its benign atmosphere, absence of attitude and straightforward sense of fun. The city also offers great variety: from salsa nights to techno clubs, from fetish bars to sports bars, and from impromptu pubs in dilapidated buildings to smart lounges with retro design. There is also a friendly and ever-evolving gay and lesbian scene. For other evening entertainment, see also *Cafés and Bars, p.30, Film, p.48* and *Music, p.80.*

LATE-NIGHT BARS

Filter Klub

Almássy utca 1; tel: 30 921-4212; www.filterclub.hu; Mon–Sat 7pm–4am; free; M2: Blaha Lujza tér, tram: 4, 6; map p.118 B1

This well-established bar caters for a range of musical tastes, from reggae to punk to indie. Evenings usually take the form of a live gig at 8pm followed by DJ sets from 10.30pm.

Jaffa

Ráday utca 39; tel: 219-5285; Mon–Thur 10am–1am, Fri 10am–2am, Sat noon–2am, Sun 2pm–midnight; free; M3: Ferenc körút, tram: 4, 6; map p.121 D2

Jaffa is one of the best of the various nightspots on Ráday utca south of the Belváros. A well-stocked bar, understated retro decor, DJs who know what they are doing, and a fun crowd form the ingredients of a good night out.

Sixtus

Nagy Diófa utca 26–8; tel: 413-6722; Mon–Fri 5pm–2am, Sat 8pm–2am; free; M2: Blaha Lujza tér, bus: 7; map p.118 A1

Quite shabby, often smoky, and, later on, very noisy: these are among the charms of this friendly bar in the Jewish quarter. After you have stoked up on the very reasonably priced drinks, there is dancing as evening turns to night.

SMS Café

Sip utca 4; tel: 30 356-4656; www.smscafe.hu; Mon–Thur 3pm–3am, Fri–Sat 3pm–6am; free except for special events; M2: Astoria, night bus: 908; map p.121 D4

This bar and restaurant may seem fairly innocuous during the day, but at night things hot up as Budapest's fetish enthusiasts congregate for boundary-pushing parties.

Most public transport services in Budapest operate from about 4.30am until 11pm. Thereafter, night buses serve many routes across the city, so getting home should not be too difficult. For details, see: www.bkv.hu/english/ejszakai/index.html.

Below: the SMS Café hosts raunchy parties.

to have on your evening's agenda. The ground floor features a stylishly retro restaurant and bar (with over 75 different cocktails), while the basement has a club with all the latest sound equipment.

Közgáz Klub

Fővám tér 8; tel: 215-4359; www.schoolclub.hu; Tue–Sat 10pm–5am; admission charge; M3: Kalvin tér, night bus: 979; map p.121 C2

Located in a cellar beneath the Economics University near Szabadság Bridge, the Közgáz is the place to come for cheap drinks, cheesy music, and a complete absence of cool – but it is nonetheless fun for all that.

Kuplung

Király utca 46; tel: 30 986-8856; www.kuplung.net; Mon–Sat 2pm–4am, Sun 5pm–4am; admission charge; M1: Opera, night bus: 923; map p.118 A1

Another of Budapest's 'ruin pubs', this time in a former bus garage. DJs perform their sets from the wreck of an old Trabant car.

Szimpla Kert

Kazinczy utca 14; www.szimpla.hu; daily noon–3am; free; M2: Astoria, tram: 47, 49, night bus: 908; map p.121 D4

This is a good example of one of Budapest's so-called 'ruin pubs' – a bar or club with temporary permission in a building that is usually awaiting redevelopment. The unrenovated fabric of the building, the rickety furniture, DIY decor and general makeshift feel of the place make for a wonderfully offbeat atmosphere. As well as the always-open bar and DJ nights, films are shown in the courtyard at the back on summer evenings.

CLUBS

Barokko Club and Lounge

Liszt Ferenc tér 5; tel: 322-0700; www.barokko.hu; Thur–Sat 5pm–late; admission charge for club; M1: Oktogon; map p.118 A2

Located on a leafy square lined with fashionable restaurants and bars, the Barokko is a good place

Below: Szimpla Kert is a quirky and uniquely-Budapest venue.

OTHER NIGHTSPOTS

A38

Pázmány Péter sétány; tel: 464-3940; www.a38. hu; Mon–Sat 11am–4am; admission charge; tram: 4, 6

A38 is an old Ukrainian barge, moored on the Pest side of the Petőfi Bridge. Its bottom deck is now used for live music acts, while there is a restaurant on the middle deck (open 11am–midnight), and DJ dance nights on the top deck.

Cinetrip

Rudas Baths, Döbrentei tér 9; tel: 356-1010; www.cinetrip. hu; admission charge; map p.120 B3

Cinetrip organises monthly club nights in one of the city's most impressive thermal bathing complexes. Events usually feature a silent film with DJs providing the soundtrack, while on occasion there are also live acts such as fire dancers and acrobats. Drinks and sandwiches are sold, and party-goers can take advantage of most of the baths' usual facilities,

including massages. Be sure, however, to bring a swimsuit, flip-flops and towel.

SEE ALSO SPAS, P.109

Gödör Klub

Erzsébet tér; tel: 20 201-3868; www.godorklub.hu; Sun–Thur noon–2am, Fri–Sat until 4am; most events free; M1, 2, 3: Deák Ferenc tér; map p.122 A4

Right in the heart of Pest is a cultural venue that offers a programme of often free events, as well as acting as a general social meeting place. There are live music events most nights, regular parties, exhibitions, studios for yoga and various kinds of contemporary dance, and monthly design markets where local designers show off their latest work.

Symbol Budapest

Bécsi út 56; tel: 333-5656; www.symbolbudapest.hu; daily 5pm–late; free; tram: 17, bus: 86

Since 2008, a grand old house in Óbuda has provided the setting for a

nightspot comprising an atmospheric cellar-restaurant, the Puskás Pancho Sports Pub screening live football, a lounge-bar, an Italian restaurant, a live music and dance club and a gallery and events space. Everything is smartly done out and beautifully maintained, and while it is clearly aimed at a well-heeled clientele, the prices are by no means astronomical.

Szilvuplé Varieté

Ó utca 33; tel: 20 992-5115; www.szilvuple.hu; Sun–Wed 6pm–2am, Thur–Sat until 4am; admission charge; M3: Arany János utca, bus: 105; map p.117 E2

This salsa and dance club occupies an impressive vaulted cellar just off Nagymező utca, in Budapest's theatre land. The well-stocked bar opens at 6pm as punters fortify themselves for the

Below: slick design at Symbol Budapest.

Left: Café Eklektika has a welcoming environment.

Gay and lesbian travellers might also find the listings on http://budapest.gayguide.net and www.budapest-gayguide.com useful for deciding where to go out in Budapest. The local edition of *Time Out* magazine (in English) also has a section on gay nightlife.

main theme of this well-established club, and the theatrical space – with balconies around a central area – forms an impressive setting. Popular with gay and heterosexual clubbers alike.

coXx Men's Club
Dohány utca 38; tel: 344-4884; www.coxx.hu; daily 9pm–4am; admission charge; M2: Astoria, tram: 47, 49, night bus: 908; map p.121 D4
This cellar bar has almost everything you could imagine: dancefloor, bunker-labyrinth, dark-room, St-Andrew cross, cages, slings and wet rooms; the club even has its own sex shop.

evening's main events at 9pm.

GAY AND LESBIAN
Alterego Bar and Lounge
Dessewffy utca 33; tel: 06 70 345-4302; www.alteregoclub.hu; Fri–Sat 10pm–4am; admission charge; M1: Opera, night bus: 914; map p.117 E2
This smartly designed bar and dance club is equally popular with Hungarians and tourists, despite (or perhaps because of) the cheesy music. Check the website for events on weekday evenings.

Café Eklektika
Nagymező utca 30; tel: 266-1226; www.eklektika.hu; admission charge; Mon–Fri 10am–midnight, Sun noon–midnight; M1: Opera, bus: 105; map p.117 E2
This lesbian-friendly café and restaurant hosts

regular DJ nights as well as live music.

Capella
Belgrád rakpart 23; tel: 06 70 295-9507; www.capellacafe.hu; Wed–Mon 10pm–4am; admission charge; M3: Ferenciek tere, tram: 2, night bus: 901; map p.122 A2
Drag shows are the

Right: packing out the bar at a Budapest club.

Palaces and Houses

The Hungarian aristocracy left their mark on Budapest with fine palaces in Baroque, neoclassical and neo-Renaissance styles. Although World War II damaged many of them, and numerous political upheavals brought about the dispersal of their contents, recent years have been kinder, with programmes of sensitive restoration. Also included in this chapter is the Parliament building – a palace built with a different purpose in mind. For other palaces and houses, see *Museums and Galleries, p.70,* and *Music, p.80.*

BUDA ROYAL PALACE (BUDAVÁRI PALOTA)

Szent György tér 2; tel: 20 4397-325; www.mng.hu; Tue–Sun 10am–6pm; admission charge; bus: 16, funicular; map p.120 A4

A castle was first built here in the 13th century by King Béla IV, and since then, numerous versions have been built and destroyed. A notable incarnation was the Italian Renaissance palace built by King Mátyás (reigned 1458–90). Its marble banqueting halls, large library, gilded ceilings, hot and cold running water, fish ponds and fountains were the stuff of legend until archaeological digs revealed their basis in fact.

Under Turkish rule from 1541, the palace fell into decline – until in 1686 it was destroyed completely as the Habsburg-led armies drove the Turks out. A new palace was subsequently built, but then replaced again with a much grander version under Maria Theresa in the later 18th century.

Above: Buda Royal Palace has been frequently rebuilt.

The 1848–9 War of Independence wrought significant damage once again, but the Compromise of the dual monarchy in 1867 heralded substantial extensions, carried out by architects Miklós Ybl, and later Alajos Hauszmann. Work was completed in 1905.

At the end of World War II, the palace was all but destroyed again. The Germans had set up their centre of operations here, and the Soviets bombarded the whole district from across the river. Reconstruction began again in 1950 and continued until the 1980s.

NAGYTÉTÉNY PALACE

Kastélypark utca 9–1; tel: 207-0005; www.nagytetenyi.hu; Tue–Sun 10am–6pm; bus: 33

One of the finest Baroque country houses in Hungary, the Nagytétény, located in the extreme southwest of Budapest, was built in the mid-18th century on the site of a succession of previous castles. It was, however, seriously damaged by fire in 1904 and then further in World War II; despite reconstruction in the immediate post-war years, it was only treated to a full and sensitive restoration in the late 1990s. Among the features that have been preserved are the murals on the upper floors. The palace now functions as a branch of the Museum of Applied Arts *(see p.77),* and displays its collection of furniture dating from about 1440 to 1850.

PARLIAMENT (ORSZÁGHÁZ)

Kossuth Lajos tér; tel: 441-4904; www.mkogy.hu/parl_en.htm;

Left: the enormous Parliament building.

There are many architecturally impressive palaces in the streets around the National Museum in Belváros. Behind the museum, at No. 10 Mihály Pollack tér, is the **Festetics Palace** (tel: 266-5222; admission only by prior arrangement), built in 1862 to designs by Miklós Ybl. The interior, with its grand staircase, ornate plaster decoration and halls of marble and mirrors, is now used for functions and events. Next door, at No. 8 is the **Esterházy family palace** (no admission), built to designs by Alájos Baumgarten in 1865. Not far away, on Károlyi Mihály utca at No. 16, is the **Károlyi Palace** (tel: 317-3611; see Petőfi Literary Museum, *p.75.* for opening times). This palace achieved its current neoclassical form after architects Anton Riegl and József Hofrichter remodelled the building in the 1830s. It is now home to a museum dedicated to the poet Sándor Petőfi, a beautifully restored library, and the Contemporary Literary Centre.

guided tours in English daily (except during parliamentary sessions) 10am, noon, 2pm; admission free for EU citizens upon proof of nationality; M2: Kossuth Lajos tér, tram: 2, bus: 15; map p.117 D2

This vast neo-Gothic parliament building – designed by Imre Steindl to emulate the British Palace of Westminster – was completed in 1902, at a cost equivalent to building a town for 30,000 people. Even today, only a small fraction of its 691 rooms is needed to accommodate the government.

Below: in an opulent Parliament chamber.

On entering, visitors make their way up a staircase of 96 steps (the Magyar state was established in 896) to the hall beneath the dome. Here, the Hungarian crown jewels are displayed in a glass case. The crown itself is said to have been a gift from the pope to St Stephen in AD1000 to mark Hungary's establishment as a Christian state. However, it is now thought that it dates from over a century after his death.

From the dome, the wing leading to the left houses the Chamber of Representatives, while to the right is the Upper House – long-since abolished, though accessible with one of the guided tours on offer. The debating chambers were designed with the latest features of the time. There was an air-conditioning system (fuelled, like the British parliament, with blocks of ice deposited in wells), and outside, on the window sills, brass racks were installed so members could leave their cigars while they were inside the chamber.

SÁNDOR PALACE

Szent György tér 1–3; no admission; funicular (sikló), bus: 16; map p.120 A4

Although originally built in the early 19th century, this neoclassical palace was almost entirely destroyed during World War II. Relatively recent renovations were completed in 2003, and the building has been used as the official residence of the president of Hungary, while also accommodating his offices.

Parks and Gardens

Budapest is blessed with several unusual parks. There is the whole of Margaret Island in the middle of the Danube, then there is Gellért Hill to the south, with its monuments and spectacular views, and perhaps most importantly of all, there is City Park (Városliget), which has its own spa, zoo, circus, museums, restaurants, and even an ice rink. Of course, there are also plenty of more conventional green spaces, where children can romp around and adults can sunbathe or play sports, depending on their energy levels. For further information on outdoor activities, see *Sports, p.110*.

CITY PARK (VÁROSLIGET)
Dósza György út; daily 24 hours; free; M1 Hősök tere, bus: 4, 20, 30, trolleybus: 75, 79; map p.118–19 B4–D3
First opened as a public park in the early 19th century, City Park hosted the celebration of the Magyar millennium in 1896. For six months, the park hosted over 200 pavilions exhibiting the best of Hungarian agriculture, commerce and culture. A few attractions – such as the Vajdahunyad Castle – survive to this day.

Entering the park from Heroes' Square, you cross a bridge designed by Gustave Eiffel over a man-made lake. In winter, it is used for ice-skating. On the far side, on an island, is Vajdahunyad Castle, housing the Agricultural Museum, Jak Chapel and monuments.

Continuing up the central avenue, on your left is the Széchenyi Thermal Baths, and, just behind, Vidám Park funfair, the circus and the Municipal Zoo. This last also has a beauti-

Above: the City Park is ideal for entertaining children.

ful Japanese garden with a fine Bonsai collection.
SEE ALSO CHILDREN, P.35; MUSEUMS AND GALLERIES, P.79; SPAS, P.109

CSEPELI STRANDFURDO PARK
Hollandi utca 14; tel: 277-6576; daily 24 hours; free; bus: 71
Among the attractions here are swimming and paddling pools, large grassy areas and playgrounds, making it popular with families.

FENEKETLEN PARK
Fadrusz utca; daily 24 hours; free; tram: 19, bus: 7
The centrepiece of this park

is a large lake with ducks and geese. Many people come here, however, to jog or use the tennis courts.

GELLÉRT HILL (GELLÉRT-HEGY) AND JUBILEE PARK (JUBILEUMI PARK)
Szent Gellért Rakpart; tel: 466-5794; daily 24 hours; free; tram: 18, bus: 27; map p.120 B2–B3
On the southern slopes of Gellért Hill, descending from the Citadel to the Gellért Hotel and Baths below, you pass through Jubilee Park, originally laid out in celebration of the 40th anniversary of the October Revolution. Winding paths are lined with flowerbeds and trees, and dotted with sculptures. There is a children's playground towards the bottom of the hill.
SEE ALSO HOTELS, P.57; SPAS, P.106

KÁROLYI GARDEN
Ferenczy Istvan utca; tel: 322-4098; daily 24 hours; free; M2: Astoria, M3: Ferenciek tere; map p.122 C2
Located just behind the

Left: the view from the landscaped Jubilee Park.

corner (tel: 263-1811; laser shows daily; admission charge).

UNIVERSITY BOTANICAL GARDENS (EGYETEMI BOTANIKUS KERT)
Illés utca 25; tel: 210-1074; www.fuveszkert.org; daily Apr–Oct 9am–5pm, Nov–Mar 9am–4pm; admission charge; M3: Klinikák

The botanical gardens (or 'Füvészkert') were originally established in 1770 to supply medicinal herbs to the medical faculty of the University of Nagyszombat. The gardens were moved several times in their history until coming to the present site in 1847.

The gardens' collection comprises some 7,000 plant species, with cacti, orchids, palms and lilies being particular specialities. Old glasshouses accommodate the tropical collection; visitors can see exotic blooms even in winter. The arboretum has up to 800 types of tree and shrub, including several Chinese Gingko trees that are 150 years old. Hungary's own flora is also well represented, with more than 400 species, organised by region and type of habitat.

For wildlife in a natural habitat, drive out just beyond the outskirts of Budapest to **Eagle Hill Nature Reserve** (Sas-hegy Természet-védelmi Terület; Tajék utca 26; tel: 408-4370; www.sas-hegy.hu; Mar–Oct Thur, Sat–Sun 10am–6pm; bus: 8). This 12-hectare (30-acre) area of limestone landscape is part of the Danube-Ipoly National Park and was one of the first nature reserves of Hungary. As well as spectacular views back towards Buda Castle, there is a wealth of flora and fauna.

Károlyi Palace, this garden square offers refuge from the hubbub of the city. You can picnic on the grass or sit on the many park benches, while children enjoy the playground.

MARGARET ISLAND (MARGIT-SZIGET) AND JAPANESE GARDEN
Daily 24 hours; free; HÉV: Margit híd, bus: 26; map p.117 C4–D4

This elongated island in the Danube is covered in parkland. As well as large areas of grass and mature trees, there are sculpture gardens, fountains, swimming pools, cycle tracks and medieval ruins. There are also a number of monuments, including the Bodor Musical Well, a water tower and a modern amphitheatre used for opera performances in the summer.

The Japanese Garden is located towards the north of the island, near the two Danubius spa hotels. Its exotic plants are laid out among streams, rock gardens, ornamental bridges and mini waterfalls.

SEE ALSO HOTELS, P.58; MONUMENTS, P.68

PEOPLE'S PARK (NÉPLIGET)
District 10; daily 24 hours; free; M3: Népliget, tram: 1

The city's largest park (about 122 hectares/277 acres) was created in the 1860s, though it benefited from a revamp not long ago. As well as trees, flowers, large open areas of grass, fountains and children's playgrounds, there is a Planetarium in one

Below: on Margaret Island.

91

Restaurants

B udapest's restaurant scene has really started to flourish in the last few years, with new places opening all the time. And while foreign influences are enriching the culture, the country's native cuisine is justly given pride of place. Moreover, as the local standard of living rises towards European averages, restaurants are engaging more and more with a discerning resident clientele rather than relying on overcharging one-off visitors from abroad. It is, of course, a recommendation of quality anywhere to see a restaurant packed full of local people. For light bite options, see *Cafés and Bars, p.30*.

CASTLE DISTRICT
21 Magyar Vendéglő

Fortuna utca 21; tel: 202-2113; daily 11am–midnight; €€; bus: 16; map p.116 B2

While many of the restaurants in the Castle District overcharge for already overpriced food of middling quality, this relative newcomer is resetting the standards. One of only four restaurants in Budapest to be awarded a Michelin Bib Gourmand (for good food at reasonable prices), it is probably the best restaurant in this area. And while still not exactly cheap, the cooking is indeed highly competent. Expect to eat goose liver, Wiener schnitzel, roast duckling, catfish and pike perch – all good solid Central European fare. The interior is in the slick modern international style; it is

Above: a classic Hungarian soup at Aranyszarvas.

comfortable but could be found anywhere.

Aranyhordó Restaurant

Tárnok utca 16; tel: 356-1367; www.aranyhordovendeglo.hu; daily 11am–midnight; €€; bus: 16; map p.116 B1

This is a decent standby for dinner in the Castle District. The traditional Hungarian cuisine is of a good standard, and the surroundings – inside a carefully restored 16th-century house – are pleasant. In the evenings, the candle-lit cellar is particularly atmospheric.

Marxim Pizzéria

Kis Rókus utca 23; tel: 316-0231; www.marximpub.hu; Mon–Thur noon–1am, Fri–Sat noon–2am, Sun 6pm–1am; €; M2: Moszkva tér; map p.116 B3

Look out for the red stars outside a restaurant on a side street near Moszkva tér. Enter inside and you are immersed in Communist-era nostalgia. First there are the flags, posters, cartoons, even barbed wire. Then there is the food: the pizzas come in varieties such as Gordi Gorbi, Red October and Pizza á la Kremlin.

National Gallery Restaurant

Budavári Palota, A-B-C-D épület, Szent György tér 2; tel: 20 4397-325; Tue–Sun 10am–6pm; €; bus: 16; map p.120 A4

If you are looking for a simple lunch – salads and wholesome Hungarian hot dishes – and do not want any fuss or great expense, then this is a good option.

Price guide for a 2-course meal with a glass of wine:
€€€ €40 or above
€€   €15–40
€   up to €15

Left: tucking in at well-established Kéhli Vendéglő.

grey catfish, lamb offal with home-made gnocchi, and buffalo tenderloin with paprika potato. At lunchtimes there is a reasonably priced set menu.

Röma Ételbár
Csalogány utca 23–4; tel: 201-4545; www.controll.hu/roma; Mon–Sat 11am–4pm; €; M2: Batthyány tér; map p.116 B2
This is how restaurants used to be in Budapest: slightly ramshackle, filled with the hubbub of a local clientele, and fragrant with the homely smells of paprika-heavy cooking. Try green-bean soup, mushroom paprika with home-made noodles, pancakes Hortobágyi-style or pork ribs fried in breadcrumbs.

ÓBUDA
Kéhli Vendéglő
Mókus utca 22; tel: 368-0613; www.kehli.hu; daily noon–11.30pm; €€; HÉV: Tímár utca, bus: 86
This restaurant is famous in Hungary as the place where novelist Gyula Krúdy (1878–1933) used to dine. He did not have far to come; his house is just round the corner at Dugovics Titusz tér 13-17. Many of the dishes on

It is customary to tip waiting staff in restaurants between 10 and 15 percent, providing that you were satisfied with the service. Some restaurants automatically add a service charge to your bill, in which case you do not need to leave any further tip.

SOUTH OF THE CASTLE DISTRICT: GELLÉRT HILL AND TABÁN
Aranyszarvas
Szarvas tér 1; tel: 375-6451; www.aranyszarvas.hu; daily noon–11pm; €€; tram: 18, 19, bus: 5, 86; map p.120 B3
Among the assets of this restaurant are the wonderful building (the historic Golden Stag House), the handy location at the foot of the Castle Hill near the Semmelweis Museum, and the picturesque terrace for dining outside in summer. The menu is Hungarian, though with a heavy French accent, and the wine list presents a good

opportunity to sample quality Hungarian wines.

NORTH OF THE CASTLE DISTRICT: VÍZIVÁROS, ROZSADOMB AND MARGARET ISLAND
Csalogány 26
Csalogány utca 26; tel: 201 7892; www.csalogany26.hu; Tue–Sat noon–3pm, 7–10pm; €€; M2: Batthyány tér; map p.116 B2
The emphasis at this informal, no-nonsense restaurant is rightly on the food, and recognition by the Michelin Guide with a Bib Gourmand award is well deserved. Dishes include sauerkraut soup,

offer remain the same as in Krúdy's day: classic Transylvanian goulash, bone-marrow soup, roast carp, goose liver fried in breadcrumbs and then strudel and pancakes for dessert.

Regi Sipos Halászkert

Lajos utca 46; tel: 250-8082; www.regisipos.hu; daily noon–11pm; €€; HÉV: Tímár út

If nothing else, it is worth coming here for the fish soup. Seventy years of tradition have gone into the making of this, and many of the restaurant's other fish recipes. And if you are that way inclined, you can even inspect specimens of fresh fish at your table before they are taken away and cooked.

LIPÓTVÁROS
Café Kör

Sas utca 17; tel: 311-0053; www.cafekor.com; Mon–Sat 10am–10pm; €€; M3: Arany János utca; map p.117 D1

This stylish restaurant translates the concept and atmosphere of a French bistro in a metropolitan Hungarian context very effectively. The bedrock of the menu is Hungarian cuisine, though some effort is made to lighten tradi-

tionally heavy dishes, and there is a noticeable French influence. Good breakfasts served until noon.

Callas

Andrássy út 20; tel: 354-0954; www.callascafe.hu; daily 10am–midnight; €€; M1: Opera; map p.117 E1

As you might guess from the name, this restaurant is located next door to the State Opera, and occupies the old ticket hall. With its Belle-Epoque fittings, vaulted ceiling and mosaic floor, it makes for a very elegant setting, whether for breakfast, lunch, afternoon tea or dinner. The meals are competently prepared, though the cakes and pastries are perhaps their speciality. On weekdays there is a reasonably priced 'business lunch'.

Csarnok Vendéglő

Hold utca 11; tel: 269-4906; Mon–Sat 9am–11pm, Sun noon–10pm; €; M3: Arany János utca; map p.117 E2

This is a useful place to bear in mind for an inexpensive lunch in the otherwise formal and pricey parliament district. It takes its name from an old-fashioned market hall

Although the practice is mercifully less and less common, there are still restaurants in Budapest that try to overcharge customers. Watch out particularly in prime tourist areas such as the Castle District and on Váci utca and Andrássy út. Sometimes restaurants pretend that there is an additional amount for tax or invent other spurious charges. The British and US embassies used to keep blacklists of the worst establishments for ripping off tourists. It is advisable to check price lists carefully before ordering, check whether service is included in the bill, and be prepared to argue with staff. In the unfortunate event that the dispute escalates, refuse to pay until the police have been called to adjudicate, keep your receipt and then complain to the tourist office.

(or *csarnok*) next door. The food and drink is standard Hungarian pub fare – beer, fried cheese, schnitzels and pancakes.

Kisharang Étkezde

Október 6 utca 17; tel: 269-3861; Mon–Fri 11.30am–6pm, Sat–Sun 11.30am–5.30pm; €; M1: Vörösmarty tér; map p.117 D1

Lunchtimes are always bustling and convivial at this diminutive restaurant located just around the corner from St Stephen's Basilica. Visitors will have to compete with eager locals for homely meals of goose-dumpling soup, schnitzels, paprika chicken and pancakes.

Left: Café Kör successfully blends French and Hungarian influences.

Above: embrace 1970s-chic at Menza.

Menza

Liszt Ferenc tér 2; tel: 413-1482; www.menzaetterem.hu; daily 10am–midnight; €€; M1: Oktogon, tram: 4, 6; map p.118 A2

Of the many fashionable bars and restaurants on this leafy square, the retro-style Menza is probably the most stylish, managing to re-create the 1970s cafeteria look with a dash of chic and comfort. It draws in a young and lively clientele, who are as enthusiastic about the extensive cocktail list as the menu of updated Central European dishes.

Okay Italia

Szent István körút 20; tel: 349-2991; www.okayitalia.hu; Mon–Fri 10am–11pm, Sat–Sun noon–11pm; €; M3: Nyugati pályaudvar, tram: 4, 6; map p.117 D3

If you have been overdosing on goulash during your stay, then have a night off and enjoy a pizza, risotto or pasta dish at this dependable and reasonably priced Italian.

Páva

Roosevelt tér 5–6; tel: 268-5100; www.fourseasons.com; Mon–Sat 6–10.30pm; €€€;
M1: Vörösmarty tér, tram: 2; map p.117 D1

This is the restaurant of the Gresham Palace Hotel; its glass front looks out on to the square and the Chain Bridge over the Danube. The style of cooking could be described as international-Italian, and combines fine ingredients, precise execution and elegant presentation.
SEE ALSO HOTELS, P.58

Szeráj

Szent István körút 13; tel: 311-6690; Sun–Thur 9am–4am, Fri, Sat 9am–5am; €; M3: Nyugati pályaudvar, tram: 4, 6; map p.117 D3

Although this large Turkish-food canteen is part of a chain, it does offer decent food at very low prices, and is open long after every other restaurant has closed. Choose from a large selection of kebabs and wraps, Turkish-style pizzas, salads and Eastern Mediterranean sweets such as baklava.

BELVÁROS
Alföldi Étterem

Kecskeméti utca 4; tel: 267-0224; www.alfoldivendeglo.hu; daily 11am–11pm; €; M3: Kálvin tér, tram: 47, 49; map p.122 C1

Step inside this restaurant and you are transported to the 'Alföld' or Great Hungarian Plain (in the southeast of Hungary). The rustic furniture, embroidered tablecloths and folk-art decor provide the fitting setting for the heart-warming peasant cuisine of that region. The goulash is perhaps the best in town, and the pork stew is stupendous. Try also the bean and ham soup, the home-made paprika bread, the Hortobagy-style pancakes and the sausages.

Borbíróság

Csarnok tér 5; tel: 219-0902; www.borbirosag.com; Mon–Sat noon–11.30pm; €€€; M3: Kálvin tér; map p.121 D2

If you want to sample the very best Hungarian produce, then this wine bar situated behind the Central Market Hall (Nagycsarnok) should be your first stop. The wine cellar offers some 60

Price guide for a 2-course meal with a glass of wine:	
€€€	€40 or above
€€	€15–40
€	up to €15

One dish visitors to Hungary should not leave without trying is goulash *(gulyás)*. Among the best places to sample this famous broth (made of paprika, beef, potatoes, other vegetables and perhaps dumplings too) are Alföldi Étterem, *see p.95*, Bagolyvár Étterem, *see p.99*, Borbíróság, *see p.95*, and Kádár Étkezde, *see below*.

different Hungarian wines to sample by the glass or quaff by the bottle. The food – including curded ewe-cheese dumplings, goose crackling, smoked knuckle of ham and fried rabbit with mushroom cream – is prepared from finest ingredients and executed with care. Prices are also very fair.

Central Market Hall (Nagycsarnok)
Fővám tér; Mon–Fri 10am–5pm, Sat 10am–2pm; €; M3: Kálvin tér; map p.121 C2
This food market should be on every tourist's itinerary, and since a visit is likely to stimulate the taste buds, dovetailing it with lunch is a good

idea. Fortunately, the gallery above the main hall accommodates a number of kiosks, stalls and self-service eateries where you can satisfy your appetites quickly and cheaply on good honest food.
SEE ALSO FOOD AND DRINK, P.52

Costes
Ráday utca 4; tel: 219-0696; www.costes.hu; Wed–Sun noon–3.30pm and 6.30-- midnight; €€€; M3: Kálvin tér, bus: 15; map p.121 D3
This is Hungary's first and only Michelin-starred restaurant. Chef Nicolas Delgado presents a brand of international haute cuisine, with the occasional nod toward the Hungarian context. Dishes such as sweetbreads, morel mushrooms and different textures of carrot are offered alongside roasted lobster with an emulsion of olive oil, coriander and lemongrass. An impressive vegetarian menu is also available, while the 'business lunch' menu allows you to sample the kitchen's art for a very affordable price.

Cyrano
Kristóf tér 7–8; tel: 226-3096; www.cyranorestaurant.info; daily 8am–midnight; €€–€€€; M1, 2, 3: Deák tér; map p.122 A3
The over-elaborate interior of this restaurant is an essay in the expensive bad taste of the post-privatisation period. It comes as a surprise then, that the cooking (modern European and Hungarian in style) demonstrates competent preparation of good ingredients. Breakfast, lunch and dinner are available, with good-value set menus at lunchtimes.

Glatt Kosher Carmel Restaurant
Kazinczy utca 31; tel: 322-1834; www.carmel.hu; Sun–Thur noon–11pm, Fri noon–2pm and the evening after Kabbalat Shabbat, Sat noon–2pm and 6–11pm; €€–€€€; M2: Astoria; map p.121 D4
Here you can feast on traditional Hungarian Jewish dishes such as veal in honey with stewed fruit and pine nuts, *cholent* (a traditional stew simmered overnight) and *flódní* (a dessert made of layers of walnut paste, poppy seeds and apples between thin layers of pastry). Note that dinner on Friday and Saturday evenings should be booked and paid for in advance.

Kádár Étkezde
Klauzál tér 10; tel: 321-3622; Tue–Sat 11.30am–3.30pm; €; M2: Astoria, tram: 4, 6; map p.118 A1
Thank goodness some things stay the same. This

Left: the Central Market Hall has many food stalls.

Right: Kádár Étkezde has retained its cosy decor.

diner has not changed in decades; both the presentation (checked tablecloths, soda siphons and bread baskets) and the tasty Hungarian-Jewish cooking have stood the test of time.

Kashmir Indian Restaurant

Arany János utca 13; tel: 354-1806; www.kashmiretterem.hu; Tue–Sat noon–4pm, 6–11pm; €; M3: Arany János utca; map p.117 D1

The owner of this restaurant, Allen Diwan, trained with Atul Kochhar (London's first Michelin-starred Indian chef), and as you might expect with this pedigree, the North Indian cuisine is a cut above the average. Numerous vegetarian dishes are available, and the buffet lunch is a particular bargain.

Klauzál Söröző Étterem

Klauzál tér 11; tel: 342-3116; daily 11am–11pm; €; M2: Astoria, tram: 4, 6; map p.118 A1

This typical *vendéglő* restaurant is just a few doors down from Kádár Étkezde. Simple pub fare

such as fried cheese and breaded chicken and noodles goes down well with a mug of beer.

Kőleves Vendéglő

Corner of Kazinczy utca 35/ Dob utca 26; tel: 06 20 213-5999; www.koleves.com; daily 11am–midnight; €–€€; M2: Astoria, tram: 4, 6; map p.121 D4

This is not the traditional concept of a Hungarian

vendéglő (pub-restaurant). The decor is light and contemporary in style, while the menu benefits from the addition of excellent vegetarian dishes, and is enriched with the influence of the locale (the Jewish quarter). A speciality on Fridays and Saturdays is Jewish baked beans with smoked goose leg.

Onyx Restaurant

Vörösmarty tér 7-8; tel: 429-9023; www.onyxrestaurant.hu; Mon–Sat noon–3pm, 6–11pm; €€€; M1, 2, 3: Deák Ferenc tér; map p.122 A3

Not content with producing wonderful cakes, the café-patisserie Gerbeaud has recently established this

Below: try top Hungarian cuisine at Kéhli Vendéglő *(see p.93)*.

Price guide for a 2-course meal with a glass of wine:	
€€€	€40 or above
€€	€15–40
€	up to €15

97

R

haute-cuisine restaurant in the same building. Openly aspiring to a Michelin star, the restaurant offers rich dishes made from luxury ingredients. The results are delicious, though not exactly cheap.

SEE ALSO CAFÉS AND BARS, P.32

Pampas Steakhouse
Vámház körút 6; tel: 411-1750; www.steak.hu; daily noon–12.30am; €€–€€€; M3: Kálvin tér, tram: 2, 47, 49; map p.121 C2
Prime cuts of beef are this restaurant's speciality. Choose from Angus, Kobe and Hungarian beef, and from various cuts and weights. Given the quality of the meat, the prices are fair.

> Types of eatery in Hungary include the *étterem*, or restaurant, serving Hungarian or international cuisine; the *csárda*, a more rustic type of place that often specialises in regional cooking; the *vendéglö*, which translates roughly as 'inn' or 'hostelry'; and the *kisvendéglö*, which is a small pub.

OKTOGON TO HEROES' SQUARE
Baraka
Andrássy Hotel, Andrássy út 111; tel: 483-1355; www.barakarestaurant.hu; daily 11.45am–3.30pm and 6.30–11.30pm; €€€; M1: Bajza utca; map p.118 B3
Unusually, this restaurant has a reputation independ-

ently of the hotel in which it is located. The fusion cuisine is imaginative and well executed. Seafood is a definite strength (remarkably so, given that Hungary is landlocked). The surroundings are formal, though elegant and calm.

SEE ALSO HOTELS, P.60

Café Bouchon
Zichy Jenő utca 33; tel: 353-4094; Mon–Sat 9am–11pm; €€; M1: Oktogon, tram: 4, 6; map p.117 E2
French and Hungarian cooking traditions are combined at this family-run bistro. Evening meals can end up on the expensive side; the 'business lunch', on the other hand, represents much better value.

Chez Daniel
Szív utca 32; tel: 302-4039; www.chezdaniel.hu; daily noon–3pm, 7–11pm; €€€; M1: Kodály körönd; map p.118 A3
Chef-restaurateur Daniel Labrosse offers a gourmet menu of sumptuous French-inspired dishes, involving liberal use of truffles, saffron, goose liver pâté, caviar and cream. It is rich food, but ideal for an occasional treat.

Falafel Faloda
Paulay Ede utca 53; tel: 267-9567; 10am–8pm, Sat 10am–6pm; €; M1: Oktogon; map p.118 A1
With deli-style counters downstairs and seating upstairs, this vegetarian establishment offers a healthier alternative to the usual Hungarian fare. There are a number of fixed-price options allowing you to pick various combinations

Left: find top-notch dining at Baraka.

Above: Bagolyvár Étterem offers good-value, rustic food.

of salads, breads, and, of course, falafels.

Szimpátia Zamat Étterem

Andrássy út 79; Mon–Fri 11am–4pm; €; M1: Kodály körönd; map p.118 B3

In an otherwise expensive part of town, this legacy from pre-capitalist days offers a good lunch with a minimum of fuss. It is set up as a self-service canteen with orange decor and orange checked tablecloths, and customers can fill up on soups and stews, schnitzels and goose legs for a very modest price.

VÁROSLIGET
Bagolyvár Étterem

Allatkerti út 2; tel: 351-6395; daily noon–11pm; €€; M1: Hősök tere; map p.118 C4

If Gundel's (just round the corner) is too expensive for your budget or too formal for the occasion, visit its sister-restaurant instead. The dishes are more rustic in style – though delicious all the same – and cost only a fraction of the price.

Gundel Étterem

Allatkerti út 2; tel: 321-3550; www.gundel.hu; Mon–Sat noon–2.30pm and 6.30pm–midnight, Sun 11.30am–2pm (brunch); €€€; M1: Hősök tere; map p.118 C4

First established in 1894, this restaurant was acquired by Károly Gundel in 1910, who made it into the country's most prestigious. It was also he who nurtured the tradition of combining French cooking techniques and styles with Hungarian ingredients, which has proved enormously influential. Today, the business is owned by restaurateur George Lang and cosmetics magnate Ronald Lauder. The food and service continue, as ever, at a high standard, though with prices to match. The good-value brunch on Sundays, therefore, is highly recommended.

Price guide for a 2-course meal with a glass of wine:
€€€   €40 or above
€€   €15–40
€   up to €15

Shopping

The range and quality of shops in Budapest are getting better all the time. While the liberalisation of the economy following the Communist period has brought enterprise, variety and consumer appetite, fortunately, as yet, the retail environment has not been swamped with large foreign chains. Indeed, there is an abundance of one-off boutiques, which makes shopping in Budapest a far more interesting experience than in many capitals. See also the following chapters of this book for further shopping: *Children, p.35*, for toy shops, *Food and Drink, p.51*, for food shops and market halls, and *Literature, p.65*, for bookshops.

ANTIQUES

Budapest has numerous local auction houses, dozens of antiques emporia and regular flea markets, large and small *(see p.104)*, to cater for all budgets and collecting enthusiasms. There is a particular concentration of antiques dealers around **Falk Miksa utca** (M2: Kossuth tér) just north of the parliament building in Lipótváros. The shops in the vicinity have clubbed together to market themselves via the website www.falkart.hu and to coordinate opening times and special events. Try **Antik Zsolnay** (www. antikzsolnay.hu) for ceramics, **BÁV**, the antiques branch of the state-run pawn shops (www.bav.hu), the **Európa Gallery** for furniture, the **Magyar-Francia Gallery** (www. magyar-franciagaleria.hu) for pictures and **Pintér Antik** (www.pinterantik.hu) – in an old World War II bomb shelter – for crystal chandeliers.

Above: upmarket shops can be found in Belváros.

Dunaparti Auction House and Gallery

Váci utca 36; tel: 266-8374; www.auctiongallery.hu; Mon–Fri 10am–6pm, Sat 10am–4pm; M3: Ferenciek tere, tram: 2; map p.122 A2

One of the city's main auction houses, this one has regular sales, mostly of paintings, the graphic arts and jewellery.

Judaica Gallery

Wesselényi utca 13; tel: 203-7639; www.judaica.hu;

Right: menoras at the Judaica Gallery.

Mon–Thur 10am–6pm, Fri 10am–2pm; M2: Astoria; map p.121 D4

This unique gallery specialises in items relating to Jewish culture: old prayer books, textiles, silverware, village pottery with Hebrew sayings, manuscripts and books.

ART GALLERIES

Karton Gallery

Alkotmány utca 18; tel: 472-0000; www.karton.hu; Mon–Fri 1–6pm; M3: Nyugati pályaudvar; map p.117 E2

This amusingly designed gallery puts on quirky exhibitions and auctions

Left: the Christmas Market at Vörösmarty tér.

a hint of retro and punk style, and are turned out in bold colours. Other labels stocked include Aquanauta, Camou, Balkan Tango, Heart and Roll, Red Aster, PUCC, Kriszta Marosi and Kati Nádasdi.

Emilia Anda
Galamb utca 4; tel: 933-9746; www.andaemi.com; Mon–Fri 11am–6pm, Sat 11am–2pm; M3: Ferenciek tere, bus: 7; map p.122 A2
Hungarian fashion designer Emilia Anda is renowned for using unconventional materials (even plastic or paper) in combination with more usual fabrics to produce highly structured, almost architectural clothes.

Fleischer Gyorgyne
Nagymező utca 7; tel: 267-4756; Mon–Fri 10am–6pm, Sat 10am–1pm; M1: Opera; map p.118 A1
For gentlemen of the old school, this shirt-maker is an essential pit stop on a visit to Budapest. For a very reasonable price (around €40 per shirt), you can have a shirt made to measure and to your

Each year, from late November to the beginning of January, an outdoor Christmas market is held on Vörösmarty tér in the centre of the city. Here you can imbibe the warmth of a glass of mulled wine and allow yourself to be tempted by the hearty Hungarian food on offer, as well as the stalls selling all kinds of craft and artisanal items. A visit in the evening is particularly atmospheric, as the stalls and a giant Christmas tree are decked with twinkling lights.

related to animation, comics or caricatures.

Knoll Gallery
Liszt Ferenc tér 10; tel: 267-3842; www.knollgalerie.at; Tue–Fri 2–6.30pm, Sat 11am–2pm; M1: Oktogon; map p.118 A2
The Austrian owner, Hans Knoll, has been exhibiting work by some of the best contemporary Hungarian artists since 1989.

Vintage Gallery
Magyar utca 26; 337-0584; www.vintage.hu; Tue–Fri 2–6pm; M2: Astoria; map p.122 C2

Situated near the National Museum, this gallery specialises in Hungarian photography. It represents a number of top contemporary photographers, but also sells fine photographs of the Modernist period.

CLOTHES AND ACCESSORIES
Eclectick
Irány utca 20; tel: 266-3341; www.eclectick.hu; Mon–Fri 10am–7pm, Sat 11am–4pm; M3: Ferenciek tere, bus: 7
Eclectick's own-brand streetwear and accessories are designed with

Below: fashionable streetwear at Eclectick.

specification. Choose from an array of different bolts of cotton and your preferred style of collar and cuff. Collect the finished article about two weeks later.

Katti Zoób

Szent István körút 17; tel: 312-1865; www.kattizoob.hu; Mon–Sat 10am–7pm, Sun 10am–4pm; M3: Nyugati pályaudvar, tram: 4, 6; map p.117 D3

The flagship store of this internationally acclaimed designer offers ready-to-wear lines as well as an haute-couture service.

The Lab

Kiraly utca 48; tel: 20 954-6055; www.thelab.hu; Mon–Fri 10am–8pm, Sat 10am–6pm; M1, 2, 3: Deák Ferenc tér; map p.118 A1

If you are looking for urban streetwear brands – such as Emerica, Oakley, Paul Frank, Ride, Skullcandy and Vans – then this is the place.

Látomás

Dohány utca 16–18; tel: 267-2158; www.latomas.hu; Mon–Fri 11am–7.30pm, Sat 11am–4.30pm; M2: Astoria, tram: 47, 49; map p.122 C3

Látomás stocks laid-back women's fashions from around 25 Hungarian labels.

Retrock Deluxe

Ferenczy István u 28; tel: 678-8430; www.retrock.com; Mon–Fri 10.30am–7.30pm, Sat 10.30am–3.30pm; M2: Astoria; map p.122 C2

A gaggle of young Hungarian designers offer their lines of retro urban fashion. As well as clothes, the store also sells an assortment of yesteryear kitsch, including old film posters, comics and cult toys.

Rubin Szorme

Dob utca 1; tel: 266-7362; www.rubinszorme.hu; Mon–Fri 9am–6pm, Sat 10am–4pm; M2: Astoria; map p.122 B3

Up-market retailer of fur coats, most of which are made in Italy.

Tisza Cipő

Károly körút 1; tel: 266-3055; www.tiszacipo.com; Mon–Fri 10am–7pm, Sat 9am–1pm; M2: Astoria, tram: 47, 49; map p.122 C3

This brand of trainers was resurrected a few years ago, capitalising on the fashion for all things retro. During the Communist period, a state-owned factory manufactured over 10 million pairs of shoes each year under this name. The new incarnation concentrates on brightly coloured trainers, fashion sportswear and accessories.

Varga Design

Haris köz 1; tel: 318-3221; www.vargadesign.hu; Mon–Fri 10am–6pm, Sat 10am–4pm; M3: Ferenciek tere; map p.122 A2

Haris köz, located just off Váci utca, harbours a number of up-market stores, and this one – selling designer Miklós Varga's creative jewellery – is one of the most interesting.

Vass

Haris köz 2; tel: 318-2375; www.vass-cipo.hu; Mon–Fri 10am–6pm, Sat 10am–2pm; M3: Ferenciek tere; map p.122 A2

Lászlo Vass makes shoes with old-world craftsmanship and style. As well as the bespoke service, there are also ranges of readymades, shoes for people with unusually large or broad feet and a limited selection for women too.

Above: designer wares at Katti Zoób.

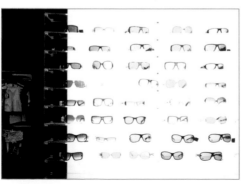

Left: trendy sunglasses can be found at The Lab.

Right: traditional dolls at
Folkart Centrum.

CRAFTS
Folkart Centrum
Váci utca 58; tel: 318-5840;
www.folkartcentrum.hu; daily
10am–7pm; M3: Ferenciek
tere, bus: 7; map p.122 B1
You can buy all kinds of
Hungarian crafts at this
shop: traditional cos-
tumes, carpets, table linen,
ceramics, icons, wood and
bone carvings, dolls, and
even musical instruments.

Holló Folkart Gallery
Vitkovics Mihály utca 12; tel:
317-8103; Mon–Fri 10am–6pm,
Sat 10am–2pm; M2: Astoria;
map p.122 B3
This charming emporium
sells good-quality hand-
made reproductions of
folk furniture, wooden
toys and ornaments, and
ceramics from different
regions of Hungary.

Originart
Arany János utca 18; tel: 302-
2162; www.originart.hu; Mon–

Perhaps Budapest's best-
known shopping street is
Váci utca, which runs roughly
north–south from Vörösmarty
tér to Fővám tér. Although
this pedestrianised street is
no longer the best place to
find a bargain, and is also
plagued with souvenir shops
and bureaux de change, it is
still, however, home to some
interesting individual stores
and is lined with many fine
buildings. As you stroll down,
look out for the florist's,
Philanthia *(see p.104)* at No.
9, the elaborately tiled facade
of No. 11 (originally for the
Thonet furniture company),
and, further down, **Folkart
Centrum** at No. 58 and the
Baroque church of St Michael.

Sat 10am–8pm; M3: Arany
János utca; map p.117 D1
The handiwork on sale
here exhibits a modern
take on naïve folk idioms.
All manner of crockery is
on offer (particularly nice
teapots), as well as figurines, pictures, clocks and
other items for the home.

DESIGN AND HOMEWARE
Forma
Ferenciek tere 4; tel: 266-5053;
www.forma.co.hu; Mon–Fri
11am–7pm, Sat 11am–4pm;
M3: Ferenciek tere, bus: 7; map
p.122 B2
Located in a passage just

Below: Váci utca has many
shops with decorative facades.

off Ferenciek tere, this is
an ideal place for buying
gifts to take back home.
There are plastic ducks
for the bath (in all different
colours), executive toys for
the office, useful gadgets
for the kitchen, and games
and puzzles for children.

Magma
Petőfi Sándor utca 11; tel: 235-
0277; www.magma.hu; Mon–
Fri 10am–7pm, Sat 10am–2pm;
M3: Ferenciek tere, bus: 7; map
p.122 B3
This chic store sells stylish
clothes and jewellery, and
items for the home – bed-
ding, paintings, ceramics,
glass, furniture, kitchen-
ware. The often colourful
and bold goods are all by
contemporary Hungarian
designers.

Printa Akadémia
Rumbach Sebestyén utca
10; no phone; www.printa.
hu; Mon–Fri 10am–7pm, Sat
11am–5pm; M1, 2, 3 Deák
Ferenc tér; map p.122 B4
Centred around this print
studio is a design shop, a
gallery and a café. As well
as T-shirts and fine prints,
there are items of home-
ware made from recycled
materials.

In Hungary, VAT (known locally as ÁFA) at up to 25 percent is added to the price of goods in shops. Non-EU visitors can reclaim the VAT on purchases over 50,000 Forints in one shop in one day. Not all shops participate in the refund scheme, but look for the Tax-free Shopping logo in shop windows. The amount a store will refund varies, though is typically 15–18 percent. To receive the refund, ask the shop assistant for a Fiscal Receipt and VAT Reclaim Form and a Tax-free Envelope, which you then take to the refund offices. There is a Global Refund counter at **IBUSZ Travel Agency** (Ferenciek tere 10; tel: 485-4119); there are also counters at airports. You will be refunded in cash, though a service charge is deducted first. Be sure to have all documentation to hand, including credit card receipts or, if you originally paid in cash, any bureau de change receipts.

ELECTRONICS AND PHOTOGRAPHY
Photo Hall
Váci utca 7; tel: 318-3005; www.photohall.hu; Mon–Fri 10am–6pm, Sat 9am–1pm; M1, 2, 3: Deák tér; map p.122 A3
For anything related to photography, this is a good

place to come. As well as selling cameras, film and accessories, computers and mobile phones, there are also scanning facilities.

FLEA MARKETS
Antik Bazár
Klauzál utca 1, tel: 322-8848; www.antik-bazar.hu; Mon–Fri 10am–6pm, Sat 10am–2pm; tram: 4, 6; map p.121 D4
Arranged over two floors, this treasure trove of retro tat is of particular interest to those in pursuit of Communist-era merchandise.

Écseri Flea Market
Nagykőrösi út 156; tel: 280-8840; www.csapi.hu; Mon–Fri 8am–1pm, Sat 6am–3pm; bus: 54
The best time to visit the city's largest flea market is on a Saturday, when all manner of junk dealers come out of the woodwork. The vast maze of alleys, corridors, shops and stalls harbours treasure such as Art Nouveau figurines (of varying quality), rustic pottery, bathroom taps, sub-Rococo furniture, Communist memorabilia, greasy mechanical parts and bad paintings. Buyers should ensure they bargain hard.

Right: the big brands are well represented in Budapest.

Petőfi Csarnok
Zichy Mihály út 14, Városliget; www.pecsa.hu; Sat–Sun 8am–2pm; tram: 1, trolleybus: 74; map p.119 D4
This fenced-off area (also known by the abbreviation PeCsa) in the far corner of City Park was intended for rock concerts. However, every weekend, in the mornings, it instead plays host to a flea market, where amateur traders dispose of the contents of their attics and professionals offload job lots and house clearances.

FLORISTS
Philanthia
Váci utca 9; tel: 266-1156; www.philanthia.hu; daily 10am–7pm; M1: Vörösmarty tér; map p.122 A3
This Secession-style shop is famed for its window displays, which are filled with puppets and toy animals arranged among exotic blooms in fairy-tale landscapes.

HEALTHCARE
Kígyó Pharmacy
Kossuth Lajos utca 2; tel: 318-5679; M3: Ferenciek tere, bus: 7; map p.122 B2
You can find this old-fashioned pharmacy under the arcades of Ferenciek tére. Apart from keeping you supplied with the usual pills, tonics, razors and condoms, it is worth a visit for the lavish Art Nouveau interior with its twinkling chandeliers.

Vision Express
Múzeum körút 11; tel: 429-

Left: stock up on local Hungarian wines.

0633; Mon–Fri 9am–6.30pm, Sat 9am–2pm; M2: Astoria; map p.122 C2
This large optician's store provides all you should need for everyday eye-care.

PORCELAIN
Herend Porcelain
Andrássy út 16; tel: 374-0006; www.herend.com; Mon–Fri 10am–6pm, Sat 10am–2pm; M1: Opera; map p.117 E1
The Herend Porcelain Manufactory has been producing delicate hand-painted wares since 1826. This shop functions as a showroom for everything from tea sets to tureens to bonbonnieres.

Zsolnay Porcelain
Margit körút 24; tel: 336-0984; http://zsolnay.com; Mon–Fri 10am–6pm; tram: 4, 6; map p.116 B3
Hungary's Zsolnay Factory, founded in 1853, is famous for its tiles made of pyro-granite and glazed in rich, iridescent colours. The factory has also adapted the material for fine

handmade, hand-painted porcelain dinner services, vases and figurines.

SHOPPING MALLS
Mammut
Lövőhaz utca 2–6; tel: 345-8020; www.mammut.hu; Mon–Sat 10am–9pm, Sun 10am–6pm; M2: Moszkva tér, tram: 4, 6; map p.116 A3
The main shopping mall in Buda is divided into two interconnected parts (Mammut and Mammut II), split over seven floors. It is occupied by Hungarian and Western European chains, including a branch of Marks & Spencer. There is a large supermarket in the basement and a food market at the back of the complex (with a fine cheese shop on the upper floor). For those less interested in retail, you can also spend your money in the cafés and restaurants, a 13-screen cinema and even a nightclub.

WestEnd City Center Mall
Váci út 1–3, 1062 Budapest;

tel: 238-7777; www.westend. hu; Mon–Sat 10am–9pm, Sun 10am–6pm; M3: Nyugati pályaudvar, tram: 4, 6; map p.117 E3
This shopping mall is the city's largest with more than 400 stores and restaurants (within a food court) plus entertainment facilities from a bowling alley to a multi-plex cinema. Access is via a tunnel from Nyugati station, and the address – just north of Lipótváros – is not to be confused with Váci utca in Belváros to the south.

One of the most eccentric shops in Budapest is **Gallwitz Pipes & Pearls** (Régi posta utca 7–9; www.gallwitz.hu; M1: Vörösmarty tér). Leopold Gallwitz started selling pipes and pearls in 1880, and the business is still going strong today. As well as selling antique and new pipes, this emporium will satisfy all your requirements for smoking paraphernalia (including tobacco), pearls, jewellery and walking sticks.

Spas

Budapest has long been the spa capital of Europe. Many of its historic state-run baths have a heritage that goes back to the period of Turkish rule, or even earlier. Some establishments, such as the Rudas or Király Baths, retain their Turkish feel, with their steam-filled atmospheres. Others, such as the Gellért and Széchenyi, are palatial complexes from the 1900's, lavishly decorated with marble, mosaics and colonnades. Most offer a wide range of treatments, from mud packing to manicures. To complement the listings below, see *Hotels, p.56,* and *Sports, p.110,* for details of other bathing establishments.

VISITING A SPA

When visiting a thermal bathing complex it is best to decide what you would like from the array of options beforehand – whether just a soak and a swim, or particular treatments or beauty therapies. Most establishments offer a standard 'swimming' ticket that allows access to the swimming pools and thermal baths. Massages, manicures, mud baths and so on cost extra, and are usually only available between, say, 9am and 6pm.

Once you have made your decision, go through the turnstile and find a cubicle to change. The attendant will usually lock the cubicle for you and give you a token to keep. Any valuables should be stowed away at the cash desk before you enter (usually for a small fee). Baths that segregate the sexes, either in different areas or on different days, do not usually require visitors to use bathing costumes (though it is a good idea

Above: one of the Gellért Hotel's swimming pools.

to have one with you just in case) and may provide instead a white cloth that ties round your waist and flaps down over your groin. For other baths (such as the non-segregated Széchenyi) you will always need your swimsuit. You should also bring shampoo, a towel, and perhaps some flip-flops too. At some swimming pools you are required to wear a cap; if you do not have one, they can usually be bought or borrowed for a small charge. It is customary to tip attendants.

In addition to the spas listed below, there are several hotels in Budapest with thermal baths. The **Danubius Health Spa Resort** on Margaret Island *(see p.58)* offers medically orientated therapies. At the **Rácz Hotel and Thermal Spa** *(see p.57)* the emphasis is on luxury and pampering in the restored 16th-century Turkish baths and health and beauty centre. Other hotels have installed their own boutique spas on a smaller scale. The magnificent Art Nouveau **Gresham Palace Hotel** *(see p.58)* has a spa centre on the top floor, with a pool, steam rooms and a sauna. The **New York Palace** *(see p.60)* has a spa and gym in its basement, which is done out to look as if it is inside an iceberg.

SPAS AND BATHS
Gellért Hotel and Thermal Baths

Szent Gellért tér 1 (entrance to baths at Kelenhegyi út 4); tel: 466-6166; www.spasbudapest.com; daily 6am–8pm (not all services are available at weekends); tram: 18, 19, 47, 49, bus: 7, 86; map p.120 C2

Left: the Rudas Baths *(see p.109)* also stages club nights.

ing. There are 13 pools: eight thermal pools, two effervescent baths and three outdoor pools – one for swimming, one with a wave machine and another for young children. You can have a carbonic acid tub-bath, herbal or aromatic baths, a 'Kleopatra' bath with milk and honey, and even a 'chocolate spa', with sugar peeling, chocolate packing and a chocolate massage. Then there are various types of massage: foot, underwater water-beam and 'hot-stone' (a shiatsu-style massage using warm stones oiled with aromatic oils).

Other treatments include pedicures, manicures, mud-packing, dental care and physiotherapy. There are also various kinds of sauna, and even a natur-ists' sun-bathing area.
SEE ALSO HOTELS, P.57

Király Baths

Fő utca 84; tel: 202-3688; www.spasbudapest.com; daily 8am–8pm, Mon and Wed women only, Tue, Thur, Fri, Sat men only, Sun mixed; M2: Batthyány tér, tram: 19, bus: 60, 86; map p.116 C3

This extravagant hotel and bathing complex was built between 1912 and 1918 on the site of Turkish baths and a 14th-century hospital before that. The architects – Artúr Sebestyén, Ármin Hegedüs and Izidor Sterk – created a typically Secessionist hotchpotch, with beehive domes and balconies decorated with lyres.

Unfortunately, just as it opened, at the end of World War I, the hotel was requisitioned by the army of Béla Kun's Communist republic. When this regime fell a few months later, the invading Romanian army took it over; and when they departed it was the turn of the counter-revolutionary forces of Miklós Horthy. Once Horthy had established himself in power, however, the Gellért was finally able to open for business, and soon became a nexus for European high society.

Sadly, the Gellért's heyday was not to last, and shelling at the end of World War II gutted the place. After the war, the exterior was restored to its original state, but the interior was replaced mostly with new fittings.

The entrance to the baths is round the corner from the hotel's main entrance, on Kelenhegyi út. Inside, you will find vaulted halls, colonnades and rooms all done out in marble or mosaic. The choices that confront you on the menu at the cash desk are bewilder-

Right: the Király Baths.

The Király Baths were created between 1565 and 1570, during the city's period of Turkish rule. They are unusual in that they do not have their own source of water – it is piped from the springs that feed the Lukács Baths to the north. The reason the Turks sited it here was that it fell within the old Buda walls and could be used even during times of siege. The neoclassical wing facing on to the street was added to the original Turkish domed baths in 1826.

Visitors today have the use of a large octagonal pool and three smaller pools, ranging in temperature from extremely hot to icy cold, so that you can alternate according to your preference. Shafts of daylight filter through the steamy haze from small openings in the dome, and the soft echo that reverberates around the rooms seems to add to the feeling of relaxation engendered by the therapeutic waters.

Other facilities and services available include underwater massage with the use of a water beam, other more conventional massages, a sauna (dry heat) and a hammam (wet heat), and foot treatments. The standard admission charge buys you a 90-minute stay. Ensure you stick to this time limit or you will be charged extra.

Lukács Baths

Frankel Leó u. 25-29; tel: 326-1695; www.spasbudapest.com; daily 6am–8pm; tram: 4, 6, 17, bus: 6, 60, 86; map p.116 C4
The springs here have been used since medieval times, when the Knights of St John and other orders built monasteries and baths in the vicinity. Much later, during the period of Turkish rule, the energy of the springs was also harnessed for producing gunpowder and for grinding wheat. The complex you see today was built in the late 19th century. A spa hotel was also built to accommodate visitors who had come for healing properties of the waters. Many of them left marble tablets on the courtyard walls expressing gratitude for their cure. In 1937, a drinking-cure hall was added. The whole complex was renovated in the late 1990s.

The Lukács has eight pools. In one courtyard is the 'fancy' pool, with a 'whirling corridor', underwater effervescence, a neck shower, water-beam back massage built into the seat banks, a whirlpool and geysers. Another courtyard has two further swimming pools. Inside are four thermal pools, and a mud and weight bath.

Services include physiotherapy, various massages (including medical, tufa and foot), a carbonic acid

Below: the hot outdoor pools at Széchenyi Baths

Right: a game of chess at the Széchenui Baths.

tub-bath, various types of sauna, mud-packing and a chocolate spa treatment.

Rudas Baths

Döbrentei tér 9; tel: 356-1322; www.spasbudapest.com; daily 6am–8pm, also Fri–Sat 10pm–4am; tram: 18, 19, bus: 7, 86; map p.120 B3

The Rudas Baths, located on the Buda side of the Elizabeth Bridge, are based around a Turkish complex, built in the 16th century. The main dome – pierced with tiny windows that allow shafts of light to filter through – shelters an octagonal thermal pool, and several smaller pools around. An extension was added in the late 19th century to accommodate a more conventional swimming pool and a sauna. There is also a drinking hall, where visitors can take the health-boosting mineral waters.

Treatments available include massages, physiotherapy and foot care. A buffet provides refreshments after your session. Cinetrip, based here, also organises club nights within the baths.

SEE ALSO NIGHTLIFE, P.86

Széchenyi Baths

Állatkerti körút 11; tel: 363-3210; www.spasbudapest.com; daily 6am–10pm (not all services are available after 7pm or at weekends); M1: Széchenyi Fürdő, bus: 4, 20, 30, trolleybus: 70, 72, 75, 79; map p.119 C4

The Széchenyi Baths are probably the most famous of the city's baths and certainly the most family-friendly. They are the ones

featured in images of bathers playing chess, with the steam rising around them *(see picture, above)*. Indeed, people use the outdoor pools even in the middle of winter, for these are the hottest baths in Budapest, with the spring water reaching the surface at a temperature of 38°C (100.4°F).

The complex was built between 1909 and 1913 by architects Győző Cziegler and Ede Dvorsáa after hot springs were discovered here in 1879. It is conceived as a neo-Baroque palace, with domes, colonnades, fountains, chequered floors and sumptuous decoration. Renovations in the 1990s have renewed its sparkle.

Facilities include five swimming pools and 13 thermal baths. These include a 'fancy' pool with water currents, bubbles and

water-beam back massage in the sitting banks.

The standard entrance ticket includes use of the gym and wellness centre, where trained instructors offer gymnastics and aqua-aerobics as well as all the usual fitness machines. Other services include mud-packing, cellulite treatments, various kinds of massage, including Thai and foot massages, dry, steam and Finnish saunas, carbonic acid tub-baths and an ice-brew machine. A buffet-restaurant overlooks the courtyard.

Outside the front of the bath buildings, there is a modern glass pavilion, the Szent István Forrás. This *ivócsarnok* (drinking hall) sells glass tankards of water direct from the spring. The minerals in the water are supposed to help your body cope with all manner of aches and pains.

Sports

Hungary has a long and distinguished sporting history, boasting the highest number of Olympic gold medals per capita of any country in the world. Sports in which Hungarians have consistently excelled include fencing, swimming, wrestling and certain athletics events. Unfortunately, the glory has faded somewhat in recent years – Hungary has not qualified for the football World Cup tournament since 1986, for example – but all the same, there remains a healthy respect for physical endeavour, as can be seen from the variety and quality of sports venues listed below.

CRICKET

The recently established Hungarian Cricket League organises matches between local sides such as the **Baggy Blues** (http://baggyblues.weebly.com), the **Danubian Kangaroos** (www.danubiankangaroos.com) and the **Royal Tigers** (www.royaltigers.hu). Consult the **Hungarian Cricket Association's** website for fixtures (www.hungary4cricket.com). There are several cricket grounds within easy distance of central Budapest by public transport.

CYCLING
Bringohinto Bicycle Rental

Hajós Alfréd sétány 1, Margitsziget; tel: 329-2746; www.bringohinto.hu; daily 8am–sunset; bus: 26
This company rents out bikes and four-wheel pedal contraptions for use on Margaret Island paths.

Budapestbike.hu

Wesselényi utca 13; tel: 30 944-5533; www.budapestbike.hu; M2: Astoria; map p.121 D4

Perhaps the most popular place in Budapest for sports is Margaret Island. Here, you can find an athletics centre, numerous swimming pools and plenty of parkland for cycling, walking or even t'ai chi. Each year at the beginning of June, the island hosts a sports festival (www.szigetisportvarazs.hu) where local sports associations get together to organise events from boat races to beach volleyball.

Budapestbike comes highly recommended. Its men's, women's and tandem bikes are maintained in top condition, and a helmet, chain and lock, and limited insurance are included in the hire fee. The company also organises guided bicycle tours, including an evening one that takes in Budapest's better nightspots.

FOOTBALL
Ferencváros

Üllői út 129; tel: 215-6023; www.ftc.hu; admission charge; M3: Népliget
Passions run high at Hun-

gary's biggest football club.

GOLF
Polus Palace Thermal Hotel and Golf Club

Kádár utca 49, Göd; tel: 27 530-500; www.poluspalace.hu; daily 8am–9pm; admission charge
This golf course – part of a five-star thermal leisure hotel resort – is the closest 18-hole course to Budapest, located some 20km (12.5 miles) to the north.

ICE SKATING
City Park Skating Rink (Városligetí Műjégpálya)

Olof Palme sétany 5; tel: 364-0013; Oct–Mar Mon–Fri 9am–1pm, 4–8pm, Sat–Sun 10am–2pm; admission charge; M1: Hősök tere; map p.118 C4

Left: cycling is very popular on Margaret Island.

slides and even a training pool for windsurfing. It is all sheltered beneath a huge plastic dome, 72m (236ft) in diameter. In the middle of the pool, there is a replica of an ancient temple.

Palatinus Baths
Margitsziget; tel: 340-4505; www.spasbudapest.com; May–Aug daily 9am–8pm; admission charge; bus: 26
This huge lido complex has seven pools fed by the island's hot springs and the capacity for 10,000 people. There is a wave machine and a water slide.

Roman Baths (Rómaifürdő)
Rozgonyi Piroska utca 2; tel: 388-9740; www.spasbudapest. com; mid-May–Aug 9am–8pm; admission charge; bus: 34, 106
Located on the site of the Roman town of Aquincum, this lido is the successor to one that was here in Roman times. The baths include water slides and a pool for younger children.

The largest artificial outdoor ice rink in Europe offers winter visitors a chance to glide around. Skates can be rented from the neo-Baroque pavilion. Special events include figure and speed skating, concerts, a visit from Santa Claus on 6 December, and, on the last day of the season, a car race on the ice.

MOTOR RACING
Hungaroring
Mogyoród; tel: 06 28 444-444; www.hungaroring.hu; admission charge
The venue for the Hungarian Grand Prix, held in August each year, is located 20km (12.5 miles) east of Budapest. Advance

tickets can be bought via www.gpticketshop.com.

SWIMMING
Alfréd Hajós Swimming Baths
Margitsziget; tel: 466-6166; Mon–Fri 6am–3pm, summer months until 5pm, Sat–Sun 6am–6pm; admission charge; bus: 26
This has two outdoor pools and an indoor one. Hajós (1878–1955) won two gold medals for swimming at the first modern Olympics, in Athens in 1896. He was also an architect and designed this building.

Aquaworld
Ramada Resort, Íves út 16; tel: 231-3760; www.aqua-world.hu; daily 6am–9.30pm; admission charge; free shuttle bus from outside the Museum of Fine Arts daily 10am, 11am, 2pm, 4pm, 5pm, 6pm, last return bus leaves Aquaworld 8pm
Aquaworld comprises pools, steam baths, water

Left: children will love the City Park Skating Rink and the Palatinus Baths.

Hungary's national stadium is the **Puskás Ferenc Stadion** or 'Népstadion' (Istvánmezei út 3–5; tel: 471-4100; box office Mon–Fri 10am–6pm; M2: Stadionok). Built in 1953 (as the Stalinist statues outside testify), it is named after footballer Ferenc Puskás, who scored 84 goals in 85 international matches for Hungary during the 1940s and 1950s. Within the same complex is the **Budapest Arena** (Stefánia út 2; tel: 422-2600; www.budapestarena.hu; box office Mon–Fri 9am–6pm, Sat 9am–2pm). This 12,500-seat indoor venue is also used for rock concerts.

Transport

Budapest is easy to get to and easy to get around. There is plenty of choice for inward flights, including several budget options, and the city is well connected on the Continental railway network, with over 50 international services arriving and departing from the city daily. In fact, many visitors choose to fly to Vienna or Bratislava and then take the direct (and inexpensive) trains into Budapest. Within the city itself, visitors are spoilt for choice, with the extensive public transport network covering trams, trolleybuses and ordinary buses, the metro and local trains.

ARRIVAL BY AIR

Budapest has one airport, **Ferihegy** (English-speaking information line, tel: 269-7000; www.bud.hu), which is located 28km (17.4 miles) southeast of the city centre. There are three terminals. Terminal 1 is used by the budget airlines, including easyJet (www.easyjet.com); terminal 2A by the Hungarian national carrier, Malév; and terminal 2B by all other airlines. The terminals have most of the usual

Taxi drivers in Budapest have been known to overcharge tourists. It is best to order a taxi in advance or else ask for an indication of how much the fare will be in advance. At the airport, **Zona Taxis** (black cars with yellow signs; tel: 365-5555; www.zonataxi.eu) charge fixed fares according to which one of four zones in the city you are travelling to. Reputable firms within Budapest itself include **Citytaxi** (tel: 211-1111; www. citytaxi.hu), **Fő taxi** (tel: 222-2222; www.fotaxi.hu) and **Taxi4** (tel: 444-4444; www.taxi4.hu).

amenities, including tourist information offices, ATM's, bureaux de change, car-hire offices, hotel reservations services, shops and places to eat.

TO AND FROM THE AIRPORT

To reach the centre of Budapest from Ferihegy by public transport, take the No. 200 bus from any of the airport's terminals to Kóbánya Kispest metro station. From there you can take the M3 line to the city centre. The last No. 200 bus leaves the airport at 11.45pm; the metro runs until 11.10pm, after which time the 909 night bus services the route into the city centre. The journey takes approximately 45 minutes.

The **Airport Minibus Shuttle** (English-speaking line, tel: 296-8555; www.airport shuttle.hu) is more expensive, but will take you from the airport to any address within the city boundaries. Tickets can either be pre-booked, or purchased from

Above: Budapest is very well connected by rail.

the Airport Shuttle desks at the airport terminals.

Trains run between Ferihegy Terminal 1 and Nyugati pályaudvar (Western Station) in Budapest. On weekdays the No. 51 service, and at weekends the No. 38, take you to the city centre in under 30 minutes. The No. 200E bus can transfer passengers to the other airport terminals.

ARRIVAL BY TRAIN

Budapest is well connected to other European cities by train, with at least a dozen direct international services

Left: a metro train pulls out of a station.

Tickets are sold at metro stations, tobacconists and travel bureaux. They can be purchased singly, as books of 10, or else there are travel cards for one, three or seven days. Tickets (but not passes) must be validated at the machines on board buses, trams and trains. Holders of a valid Budapest Card *(see Museums and Galleries, p.79)* have unlimited use of all city public transport.

DRIVING

If driving in Budapest, bear in mind that seat belts must be worn in the front and back seats, that children under eight years must have a child safety seat, and that children under the age of 12 are not allowed to sit in the front. Keep documents such as your passport, driving licence, vehicle registration document and motor insurance with you. If driving outside built-up areas during the day, you must turn on your headlights. Most importantly, it is illegal to drink any amount of alcohol and drive, or use a hand-held mobile phone when driving.

If you are intending to rent a car in Budapest, try to book it in advance. You must be aged over 21 and have a valid driver's licence and credit card. There are car-hire desks at the airport, and all the major agencies have offices in the city. Consult **www. avis.hu**, **www.budget.hu** or **www.hertz.hu** for details.

to major cities, including Vienna, Bratislava, Prague, Bucharest and Venice. Consult www.raileurope.co.uk or www.mav.hu (the Hungarian national railways website) for details.

Budapest has three main railway stations for major national and international routes. All three stations are within 45 minutes' travel from the airport and are well integrated with the other public transport networks. Most international trains arrive at **Keleti pályaudvar** (Eastern Station). Trains from **Nyugati pályaudvar** (Western Station) connect the city with towns to the east (including the historic

towns on the Danube Bend). Trains from **Déli pályaudvar** (Southern Station) head towards Lake Balaton and into the southwest of Hungary.

ARRIVAL BY COACH

A large number of coach services operate between Budapest and other European cities. See www.euro lines.com for details. The main international bus terminal in Budapest is at **Népliget** (metro: M3 Népliget).

PUBLIC TRANSPORT WITHIN BUDAPEST

Budapest has an integrated public transport system run by the Budapest Transport Authority (www.bkv.hu). There are three metro lines, trams, buses, trolleybuses and local trains (the HÉV). Most public transport services operate from about 4.30am until 11pm. Thereafter, night buses serve many routes across the city; for details, see www.bkv.hu/english/ejszakai/index.html.

Below: buses pick up where the trams leave off.

113

Atlas

The following streetplan of Budapest makes it easy to find the attractions listed in the A–Z section. A selective index to streets and sights will help you find other locations throughout the city

Map Legend

	Pedestrian area	**M**	BKF Metro
	Notable building	HÉV	Suburban rail
	Park	✈ ✈	Airport / airfield
	Hotel	🚌	Bus station
	Shopping area	❶	Tourist information
	Transport hub	✚	Hospital
	Urban area	𝕏	Windmill
	Non urban area	🗼	Lighthouse
† Y	Cemetery	⊞	Cathedral / church
	Railway	✡	Synagogue
)⋯(	Tunnel	🎭	Theatre
– – –	Ferry route	⚊	Statue / monument
🚠	Cable car / funicular railway	◗	Cave
		✉	Post Office

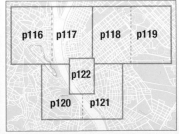

p116	p117	p118	p119
	p122		
p120	p121		

p116 | p117 | p118 | p119

p122

p120 | p121

4

RÉZMÁL

Túlipán u.

Felvinci út

Áldás u.

Eszter u.

Levél u.

Bólyai u.

Borbolya u.

Vérhalom u.

Hotel Császár

Zsigmond köz

Lukás-fürdő (Lukács Baths)

Üstökös

Aranka u.

Alvinci út

Ady Endre u.

Barsi u.

Füge u.

Szemlőhegy u.

Römer Flóris u.

Oroszi u.

Vérhalom u.

Mecset u.

Gül Baba u.

Apostol u.

Türbán

Gül Baba türbéje (Tomb of Gül Baba)

Türbe tér

GERMAN GY. PA

V. u.

Ribáry u.

Bimbó út

Zivatar u.

Kút u.

Ady Endre u.

Rózsahegy u.

Römer Flóris u.

Hotel Papillon

Margit tér

Mecset u.

Margit

Török u.

körút

Frankel Leó út

3

ORSZÁGÚT

Fillér u.

Garas u.

Marczibányi tér

Keleti Károly u.

Kisrókus u.

Ezredes u.

Bajza u.

Fillér u.

Bimbó út

Buday László u.

Polgárm Hiv.

MECHWART LIGET

M. I.

Bem József

Henger u.

Sas u.

Bes József

Forint u.

Lövőház u.

Petr. u.

Keleti Károly u.

Öntödei Múzeum (Foundry Museum)

Ganz u.

Király gyógyfürdő (Király Baths)

 Minisz

Nyúl u.

Ezredes u.

Kapás u.

Pengő u.

Fény u.

Lövőház u.

Kisrókus u.

F.E.u.

Erőd u.

Bajvívó u.

Szász K. u.

Horvát u.

Kacsa u.

Miniszterium

Városfal

Varsányi Irén u.

Vitéz

Nagy Imre tér

Sa

Erzsé temp (St Elizabeth's Chu

Erzsébet fasor

Retek u.

Margit körút

Csalogány u.

Erőd u.

Kapás u.

Csalogány u.

Gyorskocsi

2

Szamos u.

Maros u.

Ignotus u.

VÁROSMAJOR

Krisztina körút

Csaba u.

Moszkva tér

MOSZKVA TÉR M

Vérmező út

Széna tér

Ostrom u.

Hattyú u.

Fiáth J. u.

Batthyány u.

Toldy Ferenc u.

Szabó Ilonka u.

Fekete S. u.

Batthyány u.

Fazekas u.

Mária tér

Batthyány u.

Batth

VÍZIVÁROS

M. I.

Szent Anna templom

Franklin u.

Szilágyi Dezső tér

KRISZTINAVÁROS

Csaba u.

Hajnóczi u.

Maros u.

Krisztina körút

Várfok u.

Mátray u.

Logodi u.

Táncsics

Linzi u.

Levéltár

Bécsi kapu tér

Babits M. s.

Kazinczy

Hunfalvy u.

Vám u.

Toldy Ferenc u.

Vám u.

Hadtörténeti Múzeum (Military History Museum)

Magyar Jakobinusok

Kapisztrán tér

Magdolna-torony

Országház u.

Fortuna u.

Táncsics M. u.

VÁR

Hess András tér

F. köz

B.M.u.

Gimnázium u.

Nepomuki Szent János

Tem

Gyöngyi u.

Roskovics u.

Győgyfi u.

Várasmajor

Országos Onkológiai Int.

Kékk Golyó u.

Magyar Jakobinusok tere

Körút

Logodi u.

Árpád sétány

Telefónia Múzeum (Telephone Museum)

Úri u.

Szentháromság tér

Úri u.

Hilton Budapest Hotel

Kulturinnov Hotel

Mátyás templom

Szent István

Halászbástya

Corvin tér

1

N

0   400 m

0   400 yds

Ráth György u.

Kékk Golyó u.

Alkotás u.

M **DÉLI PU.**

Krisztina körút

Déli pályaudvar

VÉRMEZŐ

I

Bugát u.

Sziklakórház (Hospital in the Rock)

Lovas út

Hadik A.

Tábor u.

Labyrinth

Aranysas patikamúzeum (Pharmacy Museum)

Szirtes út

János u.

Hunyadi János út

Hajdúk hősi emlékmive

Gránit lép.

Tóth Árpád sétány

Palota u.

Dísz tér

Várszí (Castle Theatre

Attila út

Mikó u.

F.A.u.

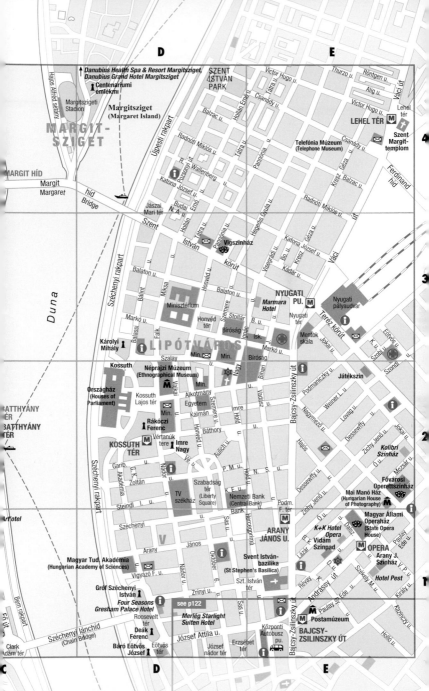

MARGIT-SZIGET

MARGIT HÍD
Margit
Margaret
Bridge

Duna

D

↑ Danubius Health Spa & Resort Margitsziget,
Danubius Grand Hotel Margitsziget
🏛 Centenáriumi
emlékmű

Margitszigeti
Stadion

Margitsziget
(Margaret Island)

SZENT
ISTVÁN
PARK

Hajós Alfréd sétány

Újpesti rakpart

Margit híd

Jászai
Mari tér

Szent

Széchenyi rakpart

E

Victor Hugo u.
Thurzo u.   Röntgen u.

Tátra u.   Alig u.   Váci út

Csanády u.   Victor Hugo u.

Balzac u.   Lehel
tér

LEHEL TÉR   Ⓜ

✉   Szent
Margit-
templom

Telefónia Múzeum
(Telephone Museum)

Ferdinánd
híd

Radnóti Miklós u.

Hollán Ernő u.

Tátra u.

Csanády u.

Katona József u.

Kresz Géza u.

Balzac u.

Hegedűs Gyula u.   Katona József u.

Pannónia u.

Radnóti Miklós u.   Váci út

Visegrádi u.   Bo... u.   Kresz   Kádár u.

Vígszínház

✉

NYUGATI
PU.   Ⓜ

Marmara
Hotel

Nyugati
tér

Nyugati
pályaudvar

Teréz Körút

ℹ

István   Körút

Balaton u.

Bálint   Miksa u.

Markó u.   Honvéd u.   Balaton u.

Szemere   Stollár

Minisztérium   Honvéd
tér   B... u.

Bíróság

Iskola u.

Markó u.

Mentők
skála

Jókai u.   Eötvös u.

K... u.   Szondi u.

Podmaniczky u.   Szondi u.

Weiner L. u.

Játékszín

ℹ

Falk   Balassi u.

Károlyi
Mihály   🏛

LIPÓTVÁROS

Szalay

Min. ✉   Min.

Min.   Nagy

Bíróság

Nagymező u.

Lovag u.

Desewffy u.

Zichy Jenő u.

Jókai u.

ℹ

Kossuth

Néprajzi Múzeum
(Ethnographical Museum)   Ⓜ

Ország ház
(Houses of
Parliament)

Kossuth
Lajos tér

Min.

Rákóczi
Ferenc   🏛

Min.

Alkotmány u.

Egyetem

Kálmán

Báthory u.

Szemere u.

Imre
Hold

Vadász u.

Bihari u.

Kolibri
Színház

Fővárosi
Operettszínház   🎭

Mai Manó Ház
(Hungarian House
of Photography)   Ⓜ

ℹ

KOSSUTH
TÉR   Ⓜ

Vértanúk
tere   🏛   Imre
Nagy

Honvéd u.

Aulich u.

Desewffy u.

Zichy Jenő u.

Ó u.

Magyar Állami
Operaház
(State Opera
House)

K+K Hotel
Opera

Vidám
Színpad

ℹ

Paulay Ede u.

Dalszí...

Széchenyi rakpart

Garib...   G. K.   Zoltán   Nádor u.   Akadémia

Steindl

TV
székház

Szabadság
tér
(Liberty
Square)

Nemzeti Bank
(Central Bank)

Hold u.   P. M. u.   Ve...   N. S. u.

Bank

Podm...
F. tér   Ⓜ

ARANY
JÁNOS U.

Hercegprímás

Lázár u.

Ⓜ   OPERA

Arany J.
Színház

Hotel Pest

Révay u.   Dalszínház u.   Ede u.   Székely M. u.   Király u.

Andrássy út

Art otel

Bem rakpart   Fő út   Széchenyi lánchíd
(Chain Bridge)

Clark
Ádám tér

Magyar Tud. Akadémia
(Hungarian Academy of Sciences)   ✉

Gróf Széchenyi
István   🏛

Four Seasons
Gresham Palace Hotel

Deák
Ferenc   🏛

Báró Eötvös
József   🏛

Széchenyi   Arany   János   Vigyázó F. u.   Nádor u.   Október...   Zrínyi u.   Sas u.

Roosevelt
tér

Eötvös
tér

Svent István-
bazilika
(St Stephen's Basilica)   🏛

Szt. István
tér

Mérleg Starlight
Suiten Hotel   ℹ

see p122

József Attila u.

Központi
Autóbusz
pu.   🚌

József
nádor tér   Erzsébet
tér   ℹ

POSTAMÚZEUM   Ⓜ

BAJCSY-
ZSILINSZKY ÚT

Postamúzeum   🏛

Bajcsy-Zsilinszky út

Kazinczy u.

Hollo u.

C   D   E

117

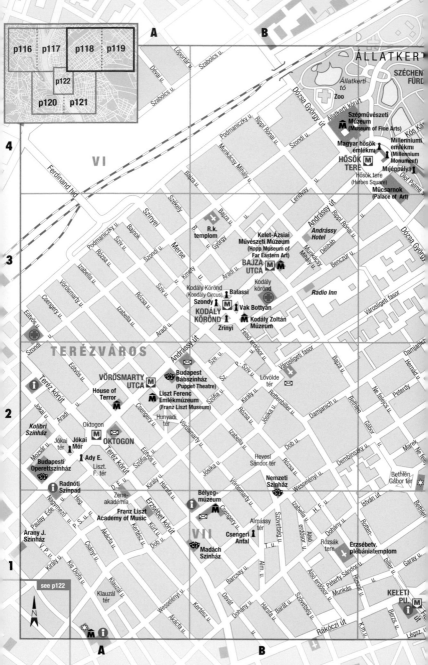

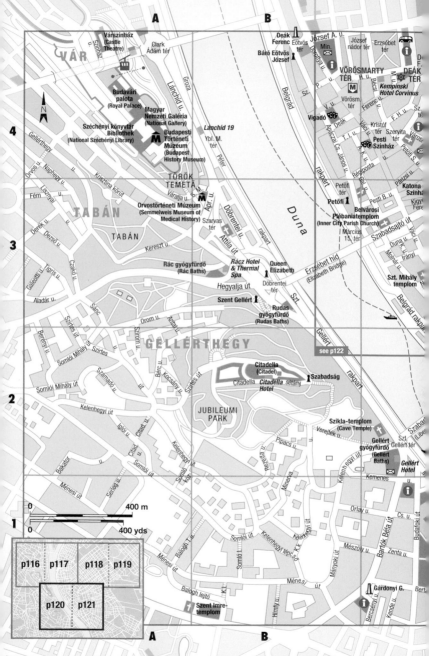

A

B

Várszínház (Castle Theatre)

VÁR

Clark Ádám tér

Lánchíd u.

Deák Ferenc

Eötvös tér

József A. u.

József nádor tér

Erzsébet tér

Báró Eötvös József

D. F.

Budavári palota (Royal Palace)

Magyar Nemzeti Galéria (National Gallery)

VÖRÖSMARTY TÉR

DEÁK TÉR

Kempinski Hotel Corvinus

4

Széchényi könyvtár Bibliothek (National Széchényi Library)

Gellérthegy

Krisztina körút

Budapesti Történeti Múzeum (Budapest History Museum)

Lánchíd 19

Ybl. M. tér

Péter

Vigadó

Kristóf tér

Szervita tér

Pesti Színház

Petőfi S. u.

TÖRÖK TEMETŐ

Váralja u.

TABÁN

Orvostörténeti Múzeum (Semmelweis Museum of Medical History)

Szarvas tér

Attila út

Döbrentei u.

Duna

Petőfi tér

Petőfi

Katona Színház

Belvárosi Plébániatemplom (Inner City Parish Church)

Márcíus 15. tér

Szabadsajtó út

3

TABÁN

Kereszt u.

Rác gyógyfürdő (Rác Baths)

Rácz Hotel & Thermal Spa

Queen Elizabeth

Döbrentei tér

Hegyalja út

Erzsébet híd (Elizabeth Bridge)

Szt. Mihály templom

Belgrád rakpart

Szent Gellért

Rudas gyógyfürdő (Rudas Baths)

Orom u.

GELLÉRTHEGY

Gellért rakpart

see p122

Citadella (Citadel)

Citadella

Citadella sétány

Citadella Hotel

Szabadság

2

JUBILEUMI PARK

Kelenhegyi út

Szikla-templom (Cave Temple)

Verejték u.

Gellért gyógyfürdő (Gellért Baths)

Gellért tér

Gellért Hotel

Pipacs u.

Minerva

Kemenes

1

0 — 400 m

0 — 400 yds

Ménesi út

Orlay u.

Bartók Béla út

Szent Imre-templom

Balogh lejtő

Gárdonyi G.

| p116 | p117 | p118 | p119 |
| p120 | p121 | | |

A

B

D

E

adách
mara
inház

Király u.

Rumbach S. u.

Holló u.

Akácfa u.

Dohány u.

New York Palace

Hársfa u.

Rákóczi út

Luther u.

Madách
tér

Károly

Elektrotechnikai
Múzeum

Wesselényi u.

Nagy Diófa u.

Klauzál u.

Polgárm.
Hiv.

Osvát u.

Kiss József u.

Bezerédi u.

Erkel
Színház

ELVÁROS

körút

gemmel-

Y.M.

Kazinczy u.

Dob u.

Síp u.

Nagy
Zsinagóga

Zsidó
Múzeum

Dohány u.

BLAHA
L. TÉR

Blaha
Lujza tér

M.E.U.

Somogyi B. u.

József körút

Bacsó B.

Atrium
Fashion Hotel

Népszínház u.

Szil. u.

4

Vármegye

Kossuth

Rákóczi út

Szentkirályi u.

Síp u.

Ódry
Színpad

Rókus
Kórház

Rókus
Káp.

Ref.
templom

Hotel
Anna

Kőfaragó u.

Bérkocsis u.

Tolnai

Aurora

Fecske u.

ASTORIA

Magyar

Múzeum körút

Puskin u.

Trefort u.

Bérkocsis u.

Gut
tér

K. u.

Rákóczi
tér

Déri M. u.

Vig u.

RENCIEK
RE

Ferences
templom

Reáltan

Ferenczy u.

Irányi
Dániel

Bródy

Henszl. u.

Sándor

Gróf Széchenyi
Ferenc

Arany J.

Pollack
M. tér

Szentkirályi u.

Horánszky u.

Mária u.

Rökk u.

Sz. K. Sal. u.

Salétrom u.

Német u.

József u.

Danubius
Hotel Astoria

VIII

3

Károlyi u.

Cukor u.

Papnövelde u.

Petőfi Irod.
Múzeum

Egyetem
tér

Kecsk. u.

Magyar Nemzeti
Múzeum
(National Museum)

R.k.
templom

R.k.
templom

M.K.
tér

Krúdy u.

József u.

Pázmány
plébánia-
templom

Horváth
M. tér

Baross u.

Józsefv.
plébánia-
templom

Szerb
aplom

Szerb u.

Veres Pálné u.

Bástya u.

Kálvin
tér

KÁLVIN
TÉR

Krály. Pál u.

Lónyai u.

Sz.
E. tér

Szabó Ervin
Könyvtár

Rev. u.

Baross u.

32-esek
tere

32-es
ezred eml.

K. S. u.

Futó u.

Vajdahunyad u.

Polgárm.
Hiv.

Református templom
(Calvinist Church)

Hotel
Zara

Inn-Side Hotel

Török
P. u.

Ráday u.

Üllői út

Erkel u.

Csep. u.

Pál u.

Mária u.

Kisfaludy u.

József körút

Nap. u.

Nap. u.

JÓZSEFVÁROS

Fővám
tér

Vámház

Piac u.

Gönczy u.

Mátyás u.

Mozi
Ház

Köztelek u.

Markus-
ovszky
tér

Tűzoltó u.

Práter u.

Corvin
Köz

Práter u.

FERENC KÖRÜT

2

Nagy Vásárcsarnok
(Central Market Hall)

Schön

Imre u.

Csarnok
tér

Mátyás u.

Czuczor u.

Iparművészeti
(Applied Arts
Museum)

Biblia
Múzeum

Kinizsi u.

Hőgyes E. u.

Üllői út

Vajdahunyad u.

Futó u.

Nagytemplom u.

Tömő u.

Pava u.

Köztraktár u.

Kinizsi u.

Polgárm.
Hiv.

Tűzoltó u.

Liliom u.

Angyal u.

Liliom u.

Berzenczey u.

Pava u.

Örökimádás
templom

Zsil u.

G. u.

Bakáts
tér

IX

1

NEHRU

PARK

Bakáts u.

Lónyai u.

Ráday u.

Ferenc körút

Tompa u.

Mester u.

Angyal u.

Tompa u.

Ferenc
tér

Berzenczey u.

Balázs Béla u.

Viola u.

budapesti
szaki
vetem

Duna

rakpart

Boráros
tér

Liliom u.

Gát u.

Tinódi u.

Viskapu u.

Bokréta u.

Viola u.

Thaly Kálmán u.

Gát u.

Lajos u.

Petőfi híd

BÓRÁROS TÉR

HÉV

Soroksári út

Ipar u.

D

E

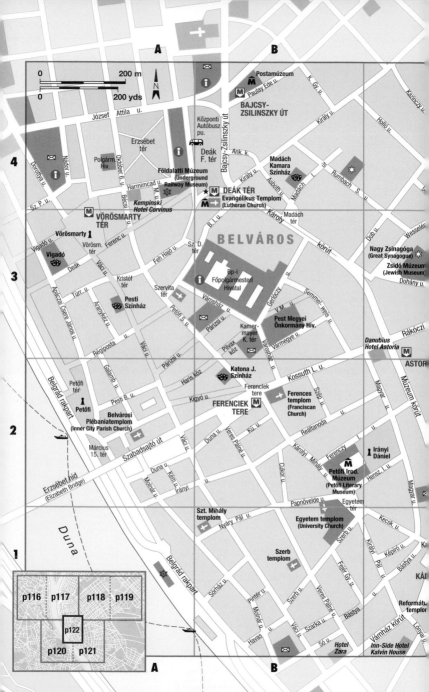

A

B

0   200 m
0   200 yds
N

József Attila u.

Postamúzeum
Ⓜ Paulay Ede u.
BAJCSY-
ZSILINSZKY ÚT

K. Gy. u.
Király u.
Holló u.
Kazinczy u.

Erzsébet tér

Központi Autóbusz pu.

🚌 Deák F. tér

Ⓜ

Polgárm. Hiv.

Nádor u.

Dorottya u.

SZ. P. u.

Becsi

Október 6. u.

Harmincad u.

ⓘ

Földalatti Múzeum (Underground Railway Museum)

Kempinski Hotel Corvinus

Madách Kamara Színház

Ank. k.

Bajcsy-Zsilinszky út

Király u.

Asbóth u.

Madách I.

Rumbach S.

Dob u.

Wesselényi u.

★ Ⓜ DEÁK TÉR
Ⓜ Evangélikus Templom
Ⓜ (Lutheran Church)

Károly Madách tér

B. u.

Károly körút

Madách tér

Ⓜ VÖRÖSMARTY TÉR

Vörösmarty ⓘ

Vigadó u.

Vigadó

Apáczai Csere János u.

Deák

Vörösm. tér

Ferenc u.

Fehér Hajó u.

Sz. D. tér

BELVÁROS

Nagy Zsinagóga (Great Synagogue)

Zsidó Múzeum (Jewish Museum)

Dohány u.

Kristóf tér

Pesti Színház

Türr u.

Váci u.

Aranykéz u.

Régiposta

Szervita tér

Bp-i Főpolgármesteri Hivatal
ⓘ

Városház u.

Szervita tér

Pilvax köz

Petőfi S. u.

✉

Kamer-mayer K. tér

Pest Megyei Önkormány Hiv.

Gerlóczy

V M. u.

Semmel-weis u.

Rákóczi út

ASTOR

Danubius Hotel Astoria
Ⓜ

Belgrád rakpart

Petőfi tér

Petőfi ⓘ

Belvárosi Plébaniatemplom (Inner City Parish Church)

Galamb u.

Pesti B. u.

Kígyó u.

Haris köz

Katona J. Színház

Ferenciek tere

FERENCIEK TERE Ⓜ

Ferences templom (Franciscan Church)

Reáltanoda u.

Kossuth L. u.

Szép u.

Magyar u.

Múzeum körút

Károlyi Mihály u.

Ferenczy

Irányi Dániel ⓘ

Petőfi Irod. Múzeum (Petőfi Literary Museum)

Henszl. u.

Magyar u.

Március 15. tér

Szabadsajtó út

Duna u.

Duna u.

Kém u.

Váci u.

Veres Pálné u.

Irány u.

Mólnár u.

Duna

Erzsébet híd (Elizabeth Bridge)

Cukor u.

Papnövelde u.

Egyetem tér

Szt. Mihály templom

Nyári Pál u.

Egyetem templom (University Church)

Szerb u.

Kecsk. u.

Királyi Pál u.

Képíró u.

Bástya u.

Ka

KÁL

Belgrád rakpart

Szerb templom

Fejér Gy. u.

Sörház u.

Pintér u.

Mólnár u.

Szerb u.

Váci u.

Szarka u.

Bástya u.

Reformátu templom

Havas

Só u.

Veres Pálné u.

✉

Hotel Zara

Inn-Side Hotel Kalvin House

Várnház körút

Lónyai u.

p116 | p117 | p118 | p119
p122
p120 | p121

A

B

122

Budapest Selective Street Index

PLACES OF INTEREST

Index

Insight Smart Guide: Budapest
Compiled by: Michael Macaroon
Edited by: Sarah Sweeney
Proofread by: Janet McCann

All Pictures by: APA/Ming Tang Evans
except: 2T/BudapestTourismBoard;
4B/Adam Jones; 4TL/Budapest
Tourism Board; 6CR/Adam Jones;
12/Andrea Puggioni; 17B/Marieke
Kuijjer; 17T/Jarita; 19T/Stephanie
Martin; 22C/Stephanie Martin; 24/25/
Dino Quinzani; 34/35T/Dollhouse;
46/47T/Budapest Tourism Board;
47B/Opethpainter; 48C/Lili Meszaros;
49B/Lili Meszaros; 56/57T/Regine
Debatty; 56C/Lanchid; 58B/Four
Seasons; 59B/Giorgio Munguzzi; 59T/
Andtor; 63B/Matthew Hunt; 66T/Paul
Mannix; 69T/Julie Lyn; 71T/Budapest
Tourism Board; 72T/Ned Richards;
74B/Procsilas Moscas; 75T/Marieke
Kuijjer; 76T/Fearless Fred; 79T/
Hungarian Snow; 80/81/Negiotiable
Me; 80C/Takato Marui; 81B/Costas
Tavernakis; 82B/Fearless Fred; 82TR/
Budapest Tourism Board; 85B/E Res;
86B/Budapest Tourism Board; 87B/

Budapest Tourism Board; 100/101T/
Budapest Tourism Board; 103B/Gillian
McLaughlin; 110/111T/Attila Magyr;
110C/Nagy David

Picture Manager: Steven Lawrence
Maps: Stephen Ramsay and
James Macdonald
Series Editor: Jason Mitchell

First Edition 2011
© 2011 Apa Publications GmbH & Co.
Verlag KG Singapore Branch, Singapore.
Printed by CTPS-China

Worldwide Distribution Enquiries:
APA Publications GmbH & Co Verlag KG
(Singapore branch)
7030 Ang Mo Kio Ave 5
08-65 Northstar @ AMK
Singapore 569880
tel: (65) 701 051/52/53
e-mail: apasin@signet.com.sg

Distributed in the UK and Ireland by:
GeoCenter International Ltd
Meridian House, Churchill Way West,
Basingstoke, Hampshire RG21 6YR;

tel: (44 1256) 817 987;
e-mail: sales@geocenter.co.uk

Distributed in the United States by:
Langenscheidt Publishers, Inc.
36–36 33rd Street 4th Floor, Long Island
City, New York 11106;
tel: (1 718) 784 0055;
e-mail: orders@langenscheidt.com

Contacting the Editors
We would appreciate it if readers would alert
us to outdated information by writing to:
Apa Publications, PO Box 7910, London SE1
1WE, UK; fax: (44 20) 7403 0290;
e-mail: insight@apaguide.co.uk